The Final Play

A NOVEL
BY LEN SPACEK

ISBN-10: 1466276126
EAN-13: 9781466276123
Library of Congress Control Number: 2011915615
CreateSpace Independent Publishing Platform
North Charleston, South Carolina

This novel is a work of fiction. The references to the schools and teams in the state of Ohio are fictional and intended to give the story a sense of reality and authenticity. Other names, characters, places, and incidents are the product of the author's imagination or are used fictitiously, and their resemblance, if any, to real-life counterparts is entirely coincidental.

For Ryan and Will.

"You learn when you get knocked down to get back up and go again. The tough will make it."
—Woody Hayes

"And in truth, I've never known a man worth his salt who in the long run, deep down in his heart, didn't appreciate the grind, the discipline. There is something in good men that really yearns for discipline and the harsh reality of head-to-head combat."
—Vince Lombardi

CHAPTER 1

June 7

"**G**o, Billy! *Go!*" shouts Jacob Conroy, as he passes me the baton.

I grab the baton and settle in behind the runner from Dayton Dunbar. Finding my stride, I zero in on the back of his blue and white uniform. My spikes dig into the rubber track as I lean into the first turn. Into the shadows from the bleachers, around the second turn at the far end of the stadium, all I can hear is the pounding of feet on the track. That second turn is a lonely place. Around the 300-meter mark, my lungs feel like they're going to explode. But one thing I've learned is to never quit—never let your teammates down. Instead, I push through the pain, grunt, and start my kick. I can hear the breath of the other runner as I pass him on the straightaway and hand off the baton to Woody Fletcher. Woody grabs the baton and flies around the first turn.

Jacob gives me a high five and says, "Way to go, man."

I bend down and put my hands on my knees to catch my breath. I've done my job. Less than fifty-two seconds later, Woody crosses the finish line with the baton raised in celebration. We win the relay and the meet.

I'm Billy Morris, the third leg in the 4 X 400 meter relay for the Unionville High School Rockets. Even though I'm only a freshman, I have the fourth-fastest 400-meter time. The quarter mile could be the toughest race in track, and in every single meet, I have to run it twice, once in the open 400 and once in the 4 x 400 relay. The 400 lets you know how tough you are, because around the 300-meter mark, you want to quit. Your legs feel like they're on fire, even when you're in good shape. But when you're running in a relay, and you're running for your friends, all that pain goes away.

Today was our last track meet. I like track, but I'm glad it's over. Now I can start to focus on the upcoming football season. In Unionville, everyone goes to the football games on Friday nights. The whole town packs the stadium like an overstuffed suitcase. It's a complete madhouse. In this town, football is more than a game. It's a way of life.

When the meet is over, I walk across the campus to catch the last few innings of my best friend's baseball game against Iron City. Jack Thompson is also only a freshman, but he's the starting pitcher on the varsity baseball team. He throws in the high 70s, low 80s, and he has a wicked splitter, better known as the Jack Thompson special. I swear the bottom drops out of that pitch. He makes most batters look stupid. Not only is Jack a great pitcher, but he can hit the hell out of the ball. When I climb to the top row of the bleachers, I see Jack in the batter's box. I know it's him because of the way his curly brown hair sticks out from under his batting helmet, and he wears his favorite number, 44. His gold number seems to glow on his royal blue uniform. He has a man on second.

Jack's dad, Mr. Thompson, yells from just behind the fence on the first-base side. His fingers shake the fence as he shouts, "Come on. Give it a ride. Show 'em what you got."

After Jack takes the first pitch for a strike, he steps out of the batter's box and turns toward the third-base coach. Jack's jaw tightens as he hits the dirt from the bottom of his cleats with his bat. I can see the frustration on Jack's face as his dad continues shouting from behind the fence.

The other parents have moved away from Mr. Thompson, who strokes his mustache and adjusts the worn-out mechanic's hat that rests on top of his bald head. His white undershirt exposes his wiry frame and Popeye-like forearms, which are covered with tattoos. A Marine Corps tattoo of a bulldog wearing a drill sergeant's hat is in plain view on his left forearm.

Jack's eyes narrow as he steps back into the batter's box. The pitcher delivers a hanging curveball. Jack steps into the pitch and crushes the ball into left field. It's a line shot, but it just keeps carrying as though it has taken flight, clearing the fence by twenty feet.

The students and parents jump to their feet and go crazy, cheering and clapping. Jack rounds the bases with smooth strides and steps on home plate, where he's mobbed by the entire team. Unionville takes the lead, 4 to 3.

Mr. Thompson shouts, "That's my boy! How 'bout that?" As he turns from the fence and pumps his fist in the air, his shin catches the bottom row of the bleachers, and he stumbles and falls to the ground.

In the stands, one parent pulls out his cell phone and says, "I've seen enough. I'm calling the police. How many times is he going to show up drunk?"

Mr. Thompson picks himself up, looks around, and brushes off his oil-stained jeans. A huge cloud of dust surrounds him, but he repositions himself along the fence as the next batter swings at a high fastball and flies out to left field to end the inning.

Jack jogs out to the mound to close out the game. He adjusts his hat over his curly brown mop, and he pounds the ball into his glove.

Mr. Thompson continues his rant from behind the fence. "Let's go! Shut 'em down! Throw 'em the heat!"

The first batter steps up to the plate. Jack throws him a curveball. The batter swings and pops it up behind home plate. The catcher moves under it and makes the catch. One out. Jack strikes out the next batter on three straight pitches. The first two pitches are fastballs, and the third pitch is a nasty Jack Thompson special that the batter swings at and misses. Two outs.

Mr. Thompson's voice rumbles through the stadium. "Look at my boy! Come on, son."

Jack's face gets more and more tense as his dad continues to yell. His next three pitches miss the strike zone. Then he throws a wild pitch in the dirt that skips past the catcher and crashes into the backstop, rattling the fence. Because he can't find his rhythm, he also walks the next batter. Jack now has a man on first and second.

Mr. Thompson roars from behind the fence. "What the hell! Come on, ump! Ain't nothin' wrong with them pitches! Open your eyes! You're costing us the game!"

The next batter hits a scorching grounder deep in the hole to the shortstop, Danny Towers, who barely knocks it down and makes a late throw to first base. The runner beats out the throw by half a step. The first-base umpire flaps his arms out to his side and shouts, "Safe! Safe!"

The bases are loaded.

Mr. Thompson stomps his feet and shouts, "He was out by a mile. You guys are blind." A Unionville police cruiser rolls up in the parking lot. Mr. Thompson turns and notices the car, but he continues his verbal assault. "Let's go, ump! Get in the game!"

Two officers climb out of their police cruiser and come up behind Jack's dad. One officer is short and skinny, and the other one looks like a husky professional wrestler. They look like David Spade and Chris Farley, but everyone knows this isn't funny. The officers approach Mr. Thompson, and the crowd's attention shifts from the game to the scene behind the fence on the first-base side. Jack looks over at his father and the two police officers and shakes his head. Mr. Thompson knows the routine. This isn't an arrest, just a cooling-off period. He is led away from the field and guided into the back of the cruiser.

Unionville's head baseball coach, Coach Logan, jogs out to the mound and says some words to Jack, pats him on the back, and returns to the dugout. Jack's next three pitches are fastballs filled with rage, probably eighty-two or eighty-three miles per hour. The dust explodes from the catcher's mitt on each pitch. The batter swings and misses all three. Unionville wins, 4 to 3.

The players from both teams walk out onto the infield and shake hands. It's a mixture of the royal blue and gold from Unionville and the red and black of Iron City. Jack grabs his glove and bat bag and walks toward me.

"Great game, bro," I say, raising my fist for a fist bump.

"Thanks." Jack half-heartedly hits my fist.

"I think that home run you crushed is still going."

He forces a smile. "The guy threw me a hanger."

While walking back toward the school, I look over at Jack and say, "What about your old man?"

"I don't know what to do. He embarrasses the hell out of me." Jack kicks a stone out in front of us.

"What can you do?"

"I tell him not to come," Jack says.

"Well, at least baseball's over," I say, trying to make my best friend feel better.

"Yeah, but then it starts all over again with football season." As we walk across the track on our way back to the school, Jack stops and looks over at me. "You know something?" Jack looks back at the baseball field where his father was just taken away by the police. "Sometimes … I wish he were dead."

When I get home, my mom is sitting at the kitchen table. She has just gotten off her shift as line manager at the Mead Paper Company in downtown Dayton. She looks up from the newspaper and says, "Hi, honey."

I can tell by the tone in her voice that something isn't right. "What's going on?" I ask.

"Billy," she says, "we need to talk." She sets the newspaper down on the table and runs her fingers through her brown hair. It needs cutting. Again.

"What about?" I ask, sensing even more concern in my mother's voice.

"Well," she begins, and then she stops herself. She closes the newspaper and shakes her head slowly from side to side. Sliding the paper to the corner of the table, she says, "Well, I've been thinking." She trails off. Then she looks up at me, into my eyes, as though she's searching for the right words. "Since your dad left, things have been tough around here. I've been putting in sixty, sometimes seventy hours a week at the factory, taking care of you and putting your sister through college." She pauses again. "And I feel like we need..."

"Need what?" I ask, my stomach turning.

"I think we need ... *I* need..." My mom nervously rubs her hands together. "You know what," she says, "let's talk about it later."

"Mom, what is it?" I ask, sensing that something isn't right.

My mom nods her head. "Yeah, let's talk about it later."

"If you say so." I head downstairs, wondering what's wrong.

CHAPTER 2
June 9

I stare at Cindy. Her bleached-blonde hair contrasts with her year-round tan. I'm convinced that I'm the luckiest kid in school. Her bright green T-shirt has a yellow lemon on the front. The shirt reads: SQUEEZE ME! And that's exactly what I want to do. I'm so into her that sometimes when I'm around her, it's hard for me to form a complete sentence, which makes me feel like an idiot. Cindy and I have been friends since elementary school, but we have just recently started dating. This has been an adjustment, for both of us.

She notices me staring, and she pushes her long blonde hair behind her ears. "Billy," she says, "would you pay attention? If you don't pass this final, you won't be able to play ball next year. Mr. Handler told you that you needed to pass this test, or you're going to fail English."

I let out a sigh. "I already looked over the study guide a hundred times. I'll be fine." This is actually the first test I have studied for all year.

Our ninth-grade English teacher at Unionville, Mr. Handler, made Cindy my study partner. I think he was playing matchmaker. Lucky for me, I didn't get Joey Fineman as a partner; that dude is so smart, he teaches computer-programming classes to adults. Instead, I got Cindy Landry. It wasn't until we were study partners this year that we started dating. She has it all: big green eyes, blonde hair, and with all the cheerleading she does in the fall, and the swimming that she does in the winter—well, let's just say she's in great shape. I'm no expert, but when I'm around Cindy, I feel like I could be in love.

On my way to see what shows are on TV, I gently push her on the shoulder, because I want to touch her. "C'mon, let's just hang out and watch a movie." I look through the list of movies that are playing. "Hey, how about *The Waterboy?*"

Cindy shakes her head. "Would you stop screwing around? This test is important. You need a good grade." Cindy is on the honor roll, and this past year she was the captain of the freshman cheerleading squad.

If it weren't for Cindy, English class would be unbearable. Forty-five minutes of English with Mr. Handler seems like an eternity. I usually sit in the back of the class and draw pictures of football players and practice writing my autograph, so it will be perfect when I become a professional running back in the NFL. I wouldn't even be studying for this test if Mr. Handler hadn't explained to me that I needed to get a good grade on the final in order to be eligible for football next year. He says I've intentionally ignored his class. Apparently my grade is hovering somewhere between a low D and an F.

I move around the basement, shooting pool and playing air hockey. As Cindy quizzes me, I stroll past her and touch her, because it's impossible for me to keep my hands off her.

While painting her fingernails some fluorescent pink color, which happens to match her toenails, Cindy goes through about twenty questions. She covers everything from John Steinbeck's *Of Mice and Men* to Harper Lee's *To Kill a Mockingbird*. When we finally finish the study guide, she asks, "Are you sure you're going to be okay on the test?"

I roll my eyes. "I knew all those answers, didn't I? I'll be fine."

She looks at her watch. "Shouldn't you call your mom and tell her you're still here? It's getting late."

"I doubt she cares. She's probably with her new boyfriend."

Cindy shakes her head and lets out a sigh. "Why are you so hard on her? You know she loves you." I hate when Cindy is right, which is pretty much all the time.

"I guess it's because my dad's not around to blame." Mom never really filled me in on the details as to why she and my dad got divorced. My old man just kind of disappeared, took a new position with his company, and moved to San Jose, California, about 2,000 miles away from Unionville, Ohio, which seems to be just fine with my mom. He sends me birthday cards that say things like, "How's it going, champ?"

Cindy applies some more nail polish. "You can't go on blaming her forever."

I line up the cue ball and sink the eight ball in the side pocket. "Yeah, I know."

"Listen, even if you don't call your mom, you still have to go. My dad says 'no boys after ten.'" Cindy takes my forearm and guides me to the steps. Did I mention that I love when she touches me?

We walk upstairs from the basement. Mrs. Landry, a stay-at-home mom, sits on their brown leather sofa. Her short brown hair turns up at her shoulders. Mr. Landry is next to her, and they are watching a *Seinfeld* rerun.

I poke my head into the living room and wave. "Goodnight," I say.

"Goodnight, Billy," they respond almost in unison, looking up from their sitcom. Without a doubt, Cindy has the All-American family.

Cindy walks outside with me and closes the door behind us. "Thanks for coming over," she says as she takes my hand. She looks toward the ground in a shy way. I love that about her.

Nodding my head, I say, "Yeah, thanks for helping me study."

"I'll see you tomorrow?"

"Yeah, tomorrow." Despite the fact that we've been friends forever, things are still awkward between us regarding the whole dating thing. She finally leans in for a kiss. I kiss her back. Her lips are wet and soft. I get dizzy, and my face turns red. I hold her tight and don't want to let go.

She releases the hug, squeezes my hands, and then turns and heads back toward the house. I look at the back of her shorts that read: ROCKETS! And then I pedal my beat-up, rusted-out, royal blue dirt bike, the Exploder, down the road. Cindy's house is only a few miles away from mine.

Because it's on my way home, I stop by Jack's house to say hello. All the lights are on, so I jump off the Exploder and walk up the driveway. As I get closer to his front porch, I hear shouting coming from an open window: Mr. and Mrs. Thompson.

"When are you going to get a job?" she shouts.

"Get off my back!" Mr. Thompson's voice explodes from the house. I can feel his voice in my bones.

She persists, "All you do is sit on that couch and drink." The television blares the ten o'clock news in the background.

Jack's voice interrupts the argument. "Mom, just let it go."

"No, I'm not done. He just sits there, every day, feeling sorry for himself, drinking until he can't see straight."

Mr. Thompson growls in his guttural voice, "I work! Been workin' on the cars in the garage. I'm just about finished rebuilding that '57 Chevy. It'll sell at the car show."

Mrs. Thompson shouts, "You've been saying that for *two years!*"

I hear a door slam, and the yelling stops. Jumping on my bike, I pedal down the dimly lit street, thinking about Jack's life. As I pass a single street lamp, my bike casts a giant shadow. I wonder how Jack deals with his dad. Sometimes I get upset that my dad isn't here, but if having him around would mean living like Jack, I guess I'm better off. Sometimes I miss my dad, wish we shared the time other kids share with their dads: playing catch in the yard, going for bike rides, doing the things dads and sons are supposed to do. I cut through our neighbor's backyard, which is lit up by our back porch light. Pulling around to the front of the house, I park my bike in the garage.

As soon as I walk into the mudroom, my mom calls from the kitchen. "Where have you been?" she asks. "It's almost eleven o'clock."

"Cindy's."

"Would you please come here?"

Annoyed, I look up from the bottom of the kitchen steps. "What?"

She drinks from a cup of coffee and reads a magazine. Looking over the top of the magazine, she asks, "Why are you home so late?"

"I was studying for my last final." I say this as though I have a million things to do, like I'm too busy to talk to my mom.

"I'm not mad. I just want to know." My mom lets out a deep breath. "You know, the minute you get home, you walk down those steps and disappear into that basement, that dungeon. I want to know how you are. I miss you." My mom puts down the magazine and runs her fingers through her hair, a sign that she is stressed. The communication between us since my dad left has almost completely shut down.

"I'm fine. School's fine," I say, as I walk down the steps to my room and flip on the light. My room is covered in posters. LeBron James is dunking on one wall, posterizing another victim. My Ray Lewis poster shows him doing that crazy dance when he comes out of the tunnel onto the field. My Emmitt Smith poster holds some of my medals and ribbons from middle-school track meets. I have a custom-made neon light that I got from my dad before he moved out. Its bright red letters shine: BILLY'S PLACE.

I brush my teeth and take out my contacts. After setting my alarm, I turn off my light and climb into bed. As I lie in bed, I think about my dad 2,000 miles away, and I wonder what it must be like for my best friend to deal with his dad. I think about what Cindy said about forgiving my mom for the divorce. And then I think about my mom and how she said that she has something important that she needs to talk about. My mind spins around and around wondering what could possibly be so important. I try to clear my mind and not think about anything, because I have a final exam tomorrow that will in many ways determine my future.

CHAPTER 3

June 10

The next morning, I wake up at 6:00 a.m. to look over my notes one last time. This is a test I know I have to pass. If I fail the test, I fail English, and that would make me ineligible for football, which just happens to be *the* most important thing in my life. My exam isn't until 9:00, and it's the last test of my freshman year of high school.

After taking a shower, I throw on my favorite Ohio State shorts and my blue and gold Unionville football shirt that boasts: PAIN IS TEMPORARY, PRIDE IS FOREVER. Putting on my tattered Cincinnati Reds hat, I grab my backpack, jump on the Exploder, and ride to school. In the center of town, the main street is lined with stores. Mr. Stams owns the Unionville market and grocery store. They make the best apple pies. On the corner is Mills' Diner, where everyone hangs out. It's the best place in Unionville to get a burger and fries. There's the local post office and Mrs. Mastadon's dress shop. The center of town is a perfect square, and in the center of that square is a little park with neatly cut grass. Sometimes in the summer, folk or jazz bands play in the ivory white gazebo. Unionville is a blue-collar town, and the people here take great pride in it.

Just north of town is Unionville High School. Friday nights in the fall, this side of town is lit up. The people of Unionville also take great pride in their football team. Jumping off my bike, I head to English class for my last exam. Walking through the halls, I call to my friend, Tombo. "What's up, buddy?"

"Hey, Billy. What's up, bro?" Tombo asks, leaning against the row of dark gray lockers.

"Hanging in there. Only one more day," I say.

"Dude, check out my new shirt." Tombo, who is a five foot nine inch fireplug with no neck, spins around and shows off his new shirt. It's black with red skulls, which isn't much different than his red shirt with black skulls. He's a clown, but because we've been friends since kindergarten, I love him like a brother.

After complimenting Tombo on his shirt, I see Cindy standing by her locker. When I get close to her, the smell of her sweet vanilla-scented perfume drives me crazy. "You ready for the test?" she asks.

"Yeah. You?" I ask, smiling.

"Of course!" Cindy rolls her eyes and playfully pushes my shoulder.

In the classroom, Mr. Handler pulls a pen from the pocket protector of his white, short-sleeved dress shirt. He looks through his Coke-bottle glasses over the class, passes out the tests and blue books, and smooths the few strands of hair that try desperately to cover his bald head. He says, "Good luck, everyone. When you're finished with the exam, put it on my desk, and you're free to go. Have a great summer!"

I start the exam like I'm in a NASCAR race. I can't wait to get it over with. The test is filled with questions from the study guide. There are questions about *Romeo and Juliet*, but I saw the movie with Leonardo DiCaprio, so I'm good there. There are questions about *Mary Shelley's Frankenstein*. I saw that one. It's the one where Robert De Niro plays the monster and Kenneth Branagh plays Dr. Frankenstein. It's actually not a bad flick. I know I did well. I've never studied harder for anything in my life. But seriously, who needs English class when Tombo's mom has just about every movie ever made? I shoot Mr. Handler a smile as I hand in my exam and step out into the hallway. I'm sure he hates me.

Jack strolls down the hall with his newest girlfriend, Leigh Hautman. She has a bar pierced through her eyebrow, and she wears blue fingernail polish. She has long brown hair, and she wears this heavy mascara that makes her eyes seem like tiny black holes. I think Jack likes her because she's a junior and older, and she drives us everywhere in her light-blue, beat-up Dodge Charger that her brother fixed up for her.

"Hey, who's finished with school this year? No longer a freshman," I say.

"I guess you are," Jack replies, trying to act cool in front of his girl.

"What are you up to?" I ask.

"Leigh and I are going to get some food. Want to go?"

"No, man. I'm going to the weight room. Coach wants us to start our summer lifting program today. I swear that guy's crazy."

"What do you expect? If he didn't blow out his knee at Notre Dame, he'd be playing on Sundays," Jack responds.

"Well, whatever, I'm going today, and so should you."

Jack takes Leigh's hand, smiles, and says, "I'll catch up with you."

Leigh barely even looks at me, turns her head, and gives me a half wave.

In the weight room, I am met by, not surprisingly, Coach Murphy. I think that dude lives there. He's a freaking monster, six feet four inches tall with broad shoulders, wavy blond hair, and unshaven, as always. He's got a huge wad of smelly chewing tobacco in his mouth, and even though he's only a few feet away from me, he shouts like he's on the other end of a football field. "Glad you could make it, Mr. Morris." He spits his tobacco into a clear plastic cup and slaps me on the back. His innocent slap sends my whole body lunging two feet forward. "Let's get you going," he says, as he grabs my folder. It has a daily workout schedule: six days a week, with weights on Monday, Wednesday, and Friday, and conditioning on Tuesday, Thursday, and Saturday. "No rest for the wicked," he grunts. And then with a mischievous grin, he says, "Mr. Morris, today I will be your personal trainer."

As he directs me to the squat rack, I think to myself, how did I get into this mess?

I step under the bar and lift it off the rack. He stands behind me and yells, "Let's go, son!" In the mirror that covers the entire sidewall, I catch the other guys from the team looking over, shaking their heads and laughing, elbowing each other and pointing at me. They are glad they are not in my shoes.

Coach Murphy shouts at me between reps. "You want to start, you gotta man up!" We go from machine to machine and work out repetition after repetition. I do preacher curls until I can't bend my arms or straighten them, military presses until I can't raise my hands over my shoulders, and leg presses until my legs feel like they're on fire.

After I finish my third set on the bench press, Coach Murphy points to the wall and grunts, "What's it say up there?"

"Hard work beats talent when talent doesn't work hard," I say, reading the words painted onto the wall in the weight room.

"That's right. Hard work beats talent every day of the week and twice on Sunday," he says. "Don't you ever forget that!"

"Yes, sir," I say. After one hour and twenty different exercises, I can't even stand up without feeling like I'm going to throw up.

The spit and tobacco in Coach Murphy's plastic cup adds to my nausea. I'm sure he sees that I'm almost dead, so he jokes, "Morris, we'll skip the plyometrics today." Because I have done so many squats, each step I take is painful. After thirty minutes of lying on the leg-press machine, I steady myself and stagger outside to my bike. I say every bad word that I know when I realize that I have about a three-mile ride home. I'm about to try to pick up my bike and just throw it in the dumpster when I see Jack and Leigh driving up in her car.

"You all right, bro?" Jack asks from the passenger seat. I must look as pale as a ghost.

"I'm not sure," I mutter back. "I just got put through the Murphy workout from hell."

Jack glances over at Leigh and says, "You think you can give him a ride home?"

"Yeah, I'll take him home," she says.

Jack gets out of the car, and I slide into the passenger seat. As Jack heads off to the weight room, he says, "I'll bring your bike to your house when I'm done."

Sinking into the soft cloth seats, I respond, "Thanks, brother."

"You doin' okay?" Leigh asks.

"Yeah, I'll be fine. I just gotta lie down."

Her blue fingertips grip the five-speed, and my whole body hurts every time the car shifts gears. Her wrists are covered by a bunch of black rubber bracelets. A yellow LIVESTRONG bracelet sticks out between all the black ones. Everybody's got something. We fly through town, going way over the speed limit and barely miss a gray Honda Civic as it turns onto a side street. Leigh looks directly at me and downshifts as she says, "You know, the whole world is based on timing."

Looking at the back end of the Honda Civic we just missed, I can't help but agree. As Leigh blasts the radio, I feel like I'm in some strange version of hell.

When Leigh slams on the brakes in my driveway, I open the door and ease myself out of the passenger seat. As I close the door, I say, "Thanks for the ride."

Without even looking in my direction, Leigh says, "No problem." She backs out of the driveway and speeds away.

Because my arms are still killing me, I have trouble pushing open the front door. Walking in the house, I slowly creep down the basement steps to my bedroom, fall face first on my bed, and crash for two hours.

When I wake up, my body aches all over. In the bathroom, I splash some water on my face and look at myself in the mirror. My brown hair is sticking straight up, and my hazel eyes squint back. While brushing my teeth, which have just recently been freed from the braces I wore for two years, I lean into the mirror with my hands on the sink. I let out a deep breath, hoping that I passed that final.

Jack has dropped off the Exploder after his workout, so I jump on the bike and ride over to Cindy's house. When I knock on the front door, no one answers, so I walk around to her backyard. Cindy is wearing a bright yellow bikini and floating on a raft in her family's pool. Did I mention that she looks amazing?

"Come on in! The water's perfect," she calls from the pool.

I throw a raft in the water and jump in. The cool water washes over my sore muscles.

Cindy swims over to me and wraps her arms around me. "So, how'd you do on the test?"

"I think I did okay."

Cindy smiles and gives me a long kiss.

We float around the pool enjoying the fact that summer is finally here, a summer that will change my life.

In the middle of the next week, I walk out to the mailbox. I've been anticipating the arrival of my report card. In fact, I haven't slept much since the last day of school. If I didn't pass that English final, my life as a football player is over. I check back toward the house to make sure that my mom isn't looking. Hiding between some bills and the *Unionville Times* is my report card from school. Quickly, I tear open the envelope and scan the grades from top to bottom. Social Studies: C, Math: C, Science: C, French: C, Art: B, Phys. Ed.: A, and finally, English: D-. I passed. Barely, but I passed. I let out a deep breath. At least I'll be eligible when football starts. I'm not proud of my grades, but school has never been a priority. It's always been second to sports. Folding the report card, I slide it into the pocket of my shorts.

CHAPTER 4

July 1

I roll out of bed and put on my shorts and a T-shirt. Three weeks into my summer routine, I start my day with fifty push-ups and one hundred sit-ups. After lacing up my running shoes, I put in my earbuds and hit the play button on my iPod. I crank my *summer training playlist*. I run my regular two-mile route, up and down the hills of my neighborhood. It's still early, so it's quiet, except for the few people in their pajamas getting their morning papers. The sun is coming up, and there's not a cloud in the sky. After my jog, I jump on the Exploder and start pedaling toward the track.

When I get just outside the track, I see someone running down the blue painted steps of the bleachers. I squint, trying to get a better view. When I get close enough, I'm surprised to see that Jack is already there running. Usually, he shows up late.

"What's up?" Jack says, bounding down the bleachers.

"What are you doing here so early?" I ask.

Jack looks away as though he's searching for the answer in the stands that surround the stadium. "My dad is having one of those days when it's best not to be around."

Motioning to the track, I say, "C'mon, a good workout will take your mind off things."

Jack nods his head. "Good idea."

We start with four hundred-meter strides, just to get our muscles loose. Then we run eight two hundred–meter sprints at almost full speed. The sun beats down, tanning our skin. We get into the grind, the hard work, the rhythm of the exercise. We run the bleachers, up and down, up and down. The truth is, I love finding out just how hard I can push myself. It's good that Jack is here. I can push him, and he makes me work harder. We end the workout with a light two-lap cool down. Summer is almost half over, and we know we don't have much more time to get ready for the season.

On the Fourth of July, Cindy, Leigh, Jack, and I go to Unionville Park, where the city is having its annual Home Days Carnival. The Ferris wheel goes around and around, the lights on the rides blink like crazy, and everyone gets their fill of cotton candy, elephant ears, and freshly squeezed lemonade.

The four of us stroll from one carnival game to another, checking out all the different things to do. At one of the booths, a giant man covered in tattoos yells out, "Four balls for a dollah! Knock down all four tahgets and win a prize!"

I want to impress Cindy, so I open my wallet and pull out a few bucks.

The carnie exposes his yellow teeth. Three are missing. "One dollah for four baseballs. You gotta knock down all four tahgets to win." He raises his eyebrows as if to say, "Suckahs."

Determined, I hand him a dollar bill. Five dollars and four tries later, I win Cindy a five-foot panda bear. The tattooed man reluctantly hands it over.

I hand it to Cindy. She gives the bear a big hug, and I get a kiss on the cheek. "Thanks," she says. "You were awesome."

"No problem," I say proudly.

While we watch a Journey cover band on the big stage, we run into Woody and Tombo and eat elephant ears. We talk about all the great times we've had coming to the Home Days festivals while we were growing up. And of course, we talk about the upcoming football season, which is right around the corner.

As the sun starts to go down, we head over to the baseball fields to watch the fireworks. After grabbing a couple of blankets from Leigh's car on the way, we find an open area in the outfield where we unfold our blankets and sit in a half circle to face the fireworks. The first few fireworks get *oohs* and *ahhs* from the crowd. The reds and blues sparkle in the blackness. Moms and dads point their fingers into the night sky as the little kids look up with wonder. Easing my arm around Cindy, I feel the warm skin on her lower back. My cold hand makes her jump, but then she settles in and melts into my arms.

The fireworks explode, and patriotic songs blare through the speakers. My best friends sit close by. Looking around the community park, I think how lucky I am to have grown up in a town like Unionville and to be surrounded by friends like Woody, Tombo, and Jack. As I get closer to Cindy, I can't help but think that everything seems right with the world.

The next evening, my mom calls from the living room. "Billy, honey, would you come here for a minute?"

Reluctantly, I make my way from the kitchen.

"How were the fireworks last night?" my mom asks, sitting in the corner of our light-green sectional sofa.

"Fine," I say, looking down at her skeptically.

She sits up straight and takes a deep, here-we-go breath. "You know, I've been thinking," she begins. This is usually not a good sign.

"About what?" I ask cautiously.

"Well, ever since your dad and I got divorced, I've been thinking about getting out of Unionville. You know, starting over."

I shift uncomfortably from one foot to the other. "What are you talking about?"

"Well, Richard and I have been talking about maybe moving, you know, somewhere warmer. He travels a lot, and most of his business is in South Carolina."

"Is this what you've been wanting to talk about?" I ask. Richard is my mom's boyfriend. Because we don't get along, I call him Dick. His dark features and his close-set eyes can be intimidating. He claims he played linebacker for the Oklahoma Sooners. He's been to a few of my freshman football games, and he criticizes the hell out of me—pointing out every little mistake. I think time has made him believe he was one of the best college linebackers ever to play at Oklahoma. I guess time makes heroes out of all of us.

My mom says, "You know, I feel like I've spent most of my life at that factory. I think a change would be good for everyone."

"What does that mean for me?"

"Well, you would go to a new school."

"What? No way. My life is here. Jack, Cindy, Tombo, and Woody, they're all here," I say, becoming defensive.

My mom shakes her head. "I'll tell you what's not fair—me getting no help from your father and having to work twelve hours a day. That's what's not fair."

"There's no way I'm leaving Unionville," I say in a more determined voice.

"Well, Richard suggested Bertram Academy. I think that might be a good idea."

"You want to send me to Bertram? To a boarding school?" My legs feel like I've just done thirty reps on the squat rack.

My mom gives me this hope-filled look. "It's a good school. I want what's best for you."

"Unionville's a good school."

My mom pulls a piece of paper out of her pocket, that I quickly recognize as my report card. "Four Cs in your major subjects and a D minus in English!" She shakes her head and says, "You've got to be kidding. You didn't bring home a book all year."

Because I know that she's right, I'm silenced. I can't even think of a good comeback.

"Bertram will give you a chance to go to a good college." My mom gets up from the couch and moves toward me.

"I can get into a good college going to Unionville."

"Bertram will give you a better chance. Richard has nothing but good things to say about it. He says Bertram has the best education around, and its sports teams are always competitive. He thinks you'd do great there."

The blood rushes to my face. "I bet he does. The farther away, the better."

My mom moves right next to me. "Why can't you just get along with him?"

"He's never said one nice thing to me. Have you ever heard him after one of my football games?"

"Sometimes you are not the easiest person to get along with. Besides, he just wants to help." My mom goes to rub my back.

I avoid her touch. "He doesn't care about me." My heart pounds in my chest, and I feel like an animal that has been backed into a corner.

Our arguing is interrupted when the doorbell rings.

My mom says, "That must be him." On her way to the door, she looks over at me. "We're going to get something to eat, and then we're going to the movies. Would you like to go?"

"I don't think so." I say this like the answer is an obvious one.

She grabs her purse from the kitchen table, and before she goes to the front door, she looks at me. "I wish you would give Richard a chance, and I want you to start thinking about Bertram."

As I storm past her on my way downstairs to my bedroom, I say, "There's no way I'm going to Bertram."

My mom gives me one of her looks and says, "Well, we'll see about that."

CHAPTER 5

August 1

The summer days are filled with workouts with Jack, weight room sessions with Coach Murphy, and afternoons in the pool with Cindy. The days rolls into weeks, and before I know it, only one week of summer vacation remains. With all the hard work I've put in, I am stronger and faster. My five foot eleven inch frame is solid, chiseled from stone. I have worked harder than ever before for this football season.

Coach Murphy says that Jack and I have the best attendance record in the weight room this summer. Jack even surprised me with how hard he's worked. He's in great shape. But recently, he's got this new mean streak, and he seems to have lost the laid-back personality that he used to have. He doesn't laugh much, or even smile for that matter. Lately, he's always on edge.

At the end of one of our lifting workouts, I ask Jack, "What's going on with you?"

"Nothing," he fires back.

"Somebody piss you off?"

Jack looks me in the eye, hesitates.

"What's up?" I ask again.

Waving me off, he says, "Nothing, I'm fine."

Shaking my head, I say, "No, man. You're totally not fine. You're my best friend. Don't you think I would know if you were fine? You haven't been right all week."

And maybe it's because we're best friends that he finally comes clean. "My mom left. This past weekend, she left."

My eyes widen. "She left? Why?"

Jack looks down. "My parents got in a huge fight."

"Dude, what happened?"

"My dad was sitting on the couch, not doing anything, like usual. My mom asked him for, like, the hundredth time when he was going to get a job. He freaked out and said that finding work wasn't easy. My mom said he was lazy and good for nothing. My dad got up and pushed her across the room, and she hit her head on the side of the door. She was bleeding. When she dabbed her head with her hand, she saw the blood. She got this terrified look on her face and ran upstairs to grab some of her stuff. Then she took off."

Trying to absorb all that Jack is telling me, I ask, "What'd you do?"

Jack takes a deep breath and collects himself. "So we got in my dad's car and went to the hospital looking for her, but she wasn't there. On the drive home from the hospital, my dad starts telling me it's my fault she left. He blames me. Can you believe that? Ever since he lost his job, he's been drinking every day. Doesn't do a damn thing but work on those stupid cars in the garage. Can you believe he blames me?"

"We gotta do something."

"Yeah, what do you suggest?"

"I don't know." I look at my best friend's slumped shoulders and tired eyes and say, "We'll figure something out."

I stop by Jack's house during our last weekend of freedom before two-a-days. His mom still hasn't come home. As I near the house, I hear shouting coming from the kitchen.

Mr. Thompson yells, "You ain't nothin'!"

I look in through the side window and see Mr. Thompson pushing Jack between taking sips from a silver beer can. "You're just a loser. You ain't never goin' to amount to nothin'." He wipes his hands on his grease-stained undershirt. "You hear me?"

Jack stands there, looks at his father, nods his head and says, "Yes, sir."

"You're lazy." He pushes Jack in the chest and fires off a few quick jabs to his rib cage and to his stomach.

Jack takes the blows. Grunting with each hit.

"Why don't you try taking your old man? Come on, Sally."

When his dad calls him Sally, Jack moves back. These words seem to pack more than the punches.

I've seen Jack punish 200-pound fullbacks and run over 220-pound linebackers. He could take down his dad and destroy him. What is it that doesn't allow us to fight an injustice within our own families?

Jack continues to back up as his father moves toward him.

"Come on, tough guy," Mr. Thompson says as he pushes Jack into the refrigerator. As Jack bounces off the refrigerator, Mr. Thompson catches him with a solid right cross to his jaw. From just outside the opened window, I can hear the pop.

Jack absorbs the punch, and he lets out something that sounds like a growl. He faces his father with a look of pure rage. Jack retaliates by pushing his father solidly in the chest and knocking him off balance, sending him crashing into the counter. Jack retreats across the kitchen, makes his way to the side door, and comes running outside. Our eyes lock.

I follow Jack down the driveway.

He looks over his shoulder at me. "What are you doing here?" he grunts in a voice I don't even recognize.

"What can I do to help?"

"Get the hell out of here. Pretend you didn't see anything." Jack continues to move away from his house.

"Get back here, boy!" Mr. Thompson shouts.

I go after Jack to help him, and more importantly, to get away from the rage that lives inside my best friend's house. "Are you okay?" I ask.

"I'm fine," says Jack.

"What about your jaw?"

Jack rubs his jaw, looks at me and says, "Don't worry about me."

CHAPTER 6

August 8

Summer vacation… is over. The first day of football practice and double sessions arrives. Players show up for the first morning practice at 7:30 a.m., rubbing the sleep from their eyes and trying to get used to getting up hours before their normal summer wake-up times.

The first hour of the first morning is spent with what Coach Murphy calls "chalk talk." He jumps right in. "Men," he explains, "the base defense we run is a 5-2. These are the different stunts out of that formation. We can blitz either the Sam or the Will linebacker. Sam is the strong-side linebacker. Will is the weak-side linebacker. We can also blitz the corners or the safeties out of this formation. When the linebacker goes outside and the defensive end shoots inside, we call that a twist stunt." It's now 8:00 a.m., and Coach Murphy throws out the words "Sam," "Will," "dart," "fire," "crash," "twist," "Okie," and "thunder." Our freshman coach kept things simple. Jack and I glance at each other and shake our heads, totally confused.

Before we start our first defensive practice, Coach Murphy says, "The depth chart explains who the starters are, who is second string, and who is third string. The positions listed here are not set in stone. They are based on seniority. This may change when the hitting starts on Friday and Saturday this week."

A chill shoots through my body as everyone hoots and hollers in anticipation of our first hit day. On the way out to practice, I look on the defensive depth chart where I see that Jack and I are both third-team linebackers behind two juniors and the two senior starters, Ron Jacobs and Willy Canter. The guys in front of us are good athletes, but Jack and I know that we can win those positions. Because we worked so hard over the summer, we feel confident.

Coach Murphy blows his whistle and brings the team together. "The next four days will be about education and repetition. Put your thinking caps on and take in everything the coaches tell you. Bring a lot of focus and energy to every drill. Do your best. One play isn't going to make or break your chances of being a starter. Be consistent. Be focused. Do your best on every single play."

The practice is like an assembly line: repetition, repetition, and more repetition. Coach Miller is our linebacker coach. He was an All-American at Ohio State. His size and goatee intimidate even the toughest players on our team.

Coach Miller starts out calmly. "This game is about hustle and hard work. As a linebacker, we work from sideline to sideline. It is imperative, absolutely necessary, that you play the ball carrier inside out." He begins to raise his voice. *"Never, never, never* get outside the running back. Don't be in a hurry. The cornerback's job is to turn the play back inside to you." His voice begins to get even louder. "If the running back cuts back against the grain and your ass is not there, you will have a seat on the bench." Soon, he is shouting. "The cornerback will do his job. You do yours!" He pauses to see if we are getting it. "Is that clear?"

We all nod our heads, more out of fear than anything else.

Coach Miller, looking confident that we understand, calms down again and continues. "Your course should be downhill, toward the line of scrimmage, no false reads, and no false steps. Read the offensive guards and mirror their steps. If your guard pulls, you pull with him. If he fires out at you, you meet him head-on. Light him up. If he doubles on the nose guard, you fire into the gap, expect the fullback trap. Men, playing linebacker is about being a warrior. It's the most important position on the defensive side of the ball." Miller has me so fired up that I feel like I can run through a brick wall.

We practice these drills over and over until they become a part of us, ingrained in us. Coach Miller shouts with an intensity that is contagious. "Practice does not make perfect. Perfect practice makes perfect! Playing linebacker requires attitude, intensity, desire, and courage! *Repetition, repetition, repetition,* until it's automatic, until you don't have to think about it."

Jack and I work together as the second group of line-backers. Coach Miller pulls Jack and me aside and says, "Keep working hard, boys."

We move on to some pass-drop drills. "Men," Coach Miller says, "when you work on your pass drops, make sure you open up to a forty-five degree angle and get to your drop zones." We work on pass drops for thirty minutes, breaking on passes, intercepting them, and sprinting back into line.

We end the defensive practice with a pursuit drill. One man is picked to be a rabbit who sprints all the way down the sideline, and we have to tag him before he reaches the end zone. We finish up with fifteen forty-yard sprints. If we dog it, we run extra. Everybody busts their butts, and then we retreat to the shade for a one-hour break.

Jack comes over to me and puts his hands up like he's ready to go a few rounds. He asks, "How you doin'?"

I raise my hands in defense. "Tireless, like I'm in the best shape of my life."

Jack fakes like he's throwing out a couple of jabs and dances from side to side. "Dude, I feel great, can't wait till we put the pads on and start hitting."

We sit in the shade and relax. Someone takes out an iPod, hooks it up to some speakers, and cranks some music. Everyone goofs around and tells stories about their summer vacation. And before we know it, the break is over.

The second session is all offense. The first half hour is instruction. Coach Murphy is very different from Coach

Miller. He patiently explains our offensive strategy. "Each player must perform his job in order for this offense to be successful. Our offense has two wide receivers, a tight end, a fullback, and a tailback." He diagrams six different plays and the blocking schemes for each play. He goes over the 34 and 35 Iso, the 38 and 39 sweep, and the 41 and 42 trap.

He finishes by saying, "The pass plays will be introduced on the third day. Running backs, be sure to hit the holes at full speed. Linemen, get to your spots with perfect technique. Offensive depth charts are on the back of the field house wall."

When the offensive instruction ends, Jack and I head to the wall and see that we are second string behind two seniors: John Phillips, the fullback, and Adam Tolliger, the tailback. John and Adam were second string last year and got into a lot of the varsity games, especially when Unionville had a big lead. John is big, at six foot one and 230 pounds, but he doesn't like to hit the way Jack does. Adam is fast, but he doesn't have my kind of speed. Plus, I'm twenty pounds heavier. I keep reminding myself that positions will be determined on hit day.

We take the field in our gold shorts, royal-blue T-shirts, and helmets. We run over the offensive plays. Coach Murphy coaches the running backs and quarterbacks. He explains the steps to the quarterbacks. Despite his knee surgery, he is super smooth. Everyone knows about his playing days at Notre Dame. He shows the steps to the tailbacks and fullbacks for each play. He says, "Make sure you have a good stance, fire out low and hard, and get to your spots at full speed. Our offense is based on timing, timing that will be perfect. Learn your playbooks. Learn the job of every player on every play."

Danny Towers started every game last year at quarterback as a junior, and he's probably expecting a great senior year. Last year, he led Unionville to the Division II state semi-final game, where the team lost to La Salle. Coach Murphy treats Danny like his own son, with unlimited patience. He must see the potential for greatness.

The offensive session lasts another hour and a half. We run the same six plays over and over, trying to perfect them. Jack and I run with the second group with Jordan Walker as our quarterback. Jordan started all the junior varsity games last year, and he led the team to a 10–0 record.

Jack and I anticipate each other's moves. We hustle, and our timing is perfect. The smile on Coach Murphy's face gets bigger and bigger after each repetition that our group executes. Being the starting tailback would be a dream come true. Ever since Jack and I were little kids playing flag football, we pretended we were the starting backfield for the Unionville Rockets. We played catch in his backyard and pretended we were playing on Friday night under the lights. We created situations: the state championship game, five seconds on the clock. I would pitch it out to him, or he would hand it off to me. We would pretend we won the state championship for the Rockets. We played until it got dark, and then we turned on the porch light until it got so dark that even the porch light wasn't enough. In eighth grade, and then in ninth grade, our dream started to take shape. In eighth grade, we were undefeated, and our freshman team dominated every team we played.

We line up for gassers at the end of practice. Gassers include running from sideline to sideline—twice. That's one repetition. We run five gassers. Backs and receivers have to run them under forty seconds; linemen have to be under fifty-five. If anyone doesn't make it in time, we have to run an extra half gasser. Two kids in our group miss, so we run a total of six gassers. But I don't care. I feel like I can run all day. After my first varsity practice, I am confident that Jack and I can be the starting backfield for the Unionville Rockets.

CHAPTER 7

August 9–11

The next two days are filled with drills, sprints, and new plays to learn. Our defensive sessions are an endless repetition of linebacker drills. Coach Miller is relentless in his quest for perfection. We do pursuit drills, read-your-guard drills, pass drops, and we work on shed-the-blocker techniques.

On offense, we put in ten plays each day. By Wednesday, we have thirty plays: twenty running plays and ten pass plays. Jack and I pick up the offense quickly. Being in great shape makes double sessions seem easy. Because we busted our butts over the summer, we spend our time learning the offense and not worrying about having to get into shape.

At the end of practice on Wednesday, Coach Murphy reminds us, "Tomorrow is our first day of pads. Friday is our first day of contact. These hitting days will be when the starters are decided."

The fourth day of practice is an acclimation day. This is the day when we get to put on all our pads and do some light hitting, if there is such a thing. Coaches start off saying it's a non-contact day, and then they laugh to each other, because almost all the drills are full go. The head coach has to follow the rules, so he structures the practice so there shouldn't be a lot of hitting. However, once we get into our individual defensive groups, the drills have the taste of full contact. Coach Miller pretends not to know what the word "acclimation" means.

Jack and I are partnered with Ron Jacobs and Willy Canter. Jack and I have never had a problem with these two guys before, but on this day, they become our enemies. We want to set the stage for the hit days, so Jack and I refuse to back down in the drills. We congratulate each other quietly when we get back into line. Ron and Willy had a great time over the summer partying, and they did not spend much time in the weight room. Their lack of conditioning is obvious during the second hour of our defensive session. Ron and Willy are constantly bent over, catching their breath. Coach Miller rides them like tired camels in the desert.

"What the hell was that?" Miller screams. "Your steps are wrong. You're out of position. That's not the technique I showed you." He chews them out for every little mistake, knowing that their errors are a result of being tired and out of shape. Coach Miller was in the weight room taking attendance every day. He knows which guys were there and which ones weren't.

During the offensive sessions, Jack and I work like crazy. The workouts on the track have built up our strength and our speed. We can run one hundred sweeps if we have to, which is more than I can say for Adam Tolliger and John Phillips. They are better off than Ron and Willy, but they don't have the stamina that Jack and I do. We run our plays at full speed. We never shy away from the contact from the scout defense; we look forward to it, invite it.

After practice, I head to the gym where Cindy and the cheerleading squad are practicing.

When her practice is over, she walks over to where I'm sitting. She wipes the sweat from her face with her shirt and says, "So, how was football?"

"Awesome. It's like pure adrenaline. I think I got a shot at starting."

Cindy smiles wide. "Well, why wouldn't you? You worked hard all summer. You deserve it."

"It's just weird. Ever since flag football, I wanted to play varsity football, and now it's here. It's just hard to believe."

We ride our bikes home, taking in a perfect summer day. At Cindy's house, we splash each other in the pool, grab each other, and tease each other. I want to kiss her, but I'm sure I saw her mom watching out the window.

That night I call Jack on my cell phone, wondering who Coach Murphy will match us up against in the hitting drills.

"Dude, I'm so jacked up," I say.

Jack responds, "We're going to pound 'em."

"Some of those seniors can barely even get through the agility drills."

"You know Murphy is going to pair us up against the starters," Jack says.

"We can beat 'em," I say confidently. "Would you want it any other way?"

"No. They don't want it like we do."

The intensity in Jack's voice gets my adrenaline pumping. "You got that right. But still, I'm nervous as hell." Along with the adrenaline, the nerves start setting in.

"Yeah, me, too, but we can do it. We can beat those guys. We've worked harder than they did. They might be older, but they're not better," Jack assures me.

I can feel my confidence growing. "Tomorrow, we're going to show Murphy and Miller that we deserve to be starters."

"Absolutely, we're going to kick some ass."

"I can't wait. I'll see you tomorrow," I say to Jack.

"Get ready, bro," he says, and he hangs up the phone.

I know that Jack and I will be paired up against the first-string linebackers and the first-string running backs. We know, given the opportunity, we can prove to the coaches that we deserve those positions. Starting on offense and defense is our goal. I toss and turn all night in bed, anticipating my first varsity hit day.

Chalk talk is brief. Coach Murphy grunts, "Our focus for today is to see who is not afraid to hit."

While we are stretching, the coaches set up cones and pads for different hitting drills, such as hamburger, pursuit drills, and 1-on-1 Iso drills. These are the same drills we've been doing since eighth grade.

In hamburger, both players lay on their backs. The offensive player is the ball carrier; the defensive player is the tackler. When the whistle blows, both players get to their feet as fast as they can, and there is a violent collision. I think it's just to find out who's tougher, who wants it more.

In the first drill, Jack goes up against Ron Jacobs. Jack is on D. He lies on his back, knees bent, with his fingers twitching with anticipation. There is an eerie silence, and when the whistle blows, Jack springs to his feet like a cat. Ron is slower getting up. When Ron lifts his head, Jack solidly plants his facemask on Ron's sternum. There is a loud "pop" of the pads. With perfect form, he lifts Ron off the ground. I swear they are five feet in the air, and Jack drives Ron backward, slamming him into the ground. There are numerous *oohs* and *ahhs* from the players, who have formed an expectant circle around the drill.

Coach Miller gives Coach Murphy a look that says, "I told you so."

Coach Murphy calls out, "Billy Morris and Willy Canter. Let's go! Let's see who wants it."

Jack, Woody, and Tombo shout words of encouragement. "Come on, Billy. Light him up! Show him what you got."

Willy's friends join in. "Let's go, Willy! Let's go, baby!"

In this drill, I play the running back, and Willy is the tackler. When the whistle blows, I spring to my feet. With a pure surge of adrenaline, I lower my shoulder behind a full head of steam. Willy doesn't get low enough and catches the brunt of the collision. There is a dull thud as I run over Willy and head into the end zone. Willy stays on the ground gasping for breath. The coaches go over to him. They unsnap his chinstrap and remove his helmet to help him get some air. About a minute later, Willy finally catches his breath and rises to one knee.

I want to go again. I know that no one can stop me. Jack and I destroy our opponents in each drill. Toward the end of the drills, Coach Murphy opens them up to anyone who feels like they have something to prove to the coaches. Jack and I look at each other and jump in drill after drill. It gets to the point where no one on the team will get across from either one of us.

Finally, Jack and I face each other. Jack is the ball carrier. He lowers his shoulder, and there is an explosion when we collide. There is a loud grunt as the contact takes us over the bags that contain the drill. Our bodies fly over the bags and go crashing into the crowd of bodies that surround us. The players on the team want blood. It's primitive, tribal. I devour it. I eat it up. It's what I've become. And the best part about it is that my best friend is no different.

In the next drill, I carry the ball, and Jack and I lower our heads at the same time. The hit is helmet to helmet. My mind goes blank and a tiny white light zooms to the center of my brain. I stagger and fall back. I've never been hit this hard. Regaining my senses, I jump back in the next drill. Jack and I go at it four times in a row, two best friends in a vicious battle. The popping from the pads echoes through the practice field. We both refuse to back down. The collisions are intense and violent, a crashing of helmets and shoulder pads. Jack runs the ball hard, and I tackle him like he's my worst enemy. Jack tackles me like he's trying to earn a position. After a while the cheering dies down; the coaches and players stand in awe. They haven't seen this kind of intensity for a long, long time. Jack and I are sweating and bruised, but tireless. The grass between the blocking bags is torn up from the action. Today, we have made a statement. And, more importantly, we have shown that no position is safe.

Coach Murphy blows his whistle and brings the team together. He spits his chewing tobacco on the ground and says, "New depth charts will be posted tomorrow. You boys did a fine job today. And if you feel like you didn't have your best stuff today, there will be future opportunities to show how bad you want it." He looks over the team and taps his pen on his clipboard. "And just so you guys know, there will be some changes based on the hitting drills from today." He blows his whistle and yells, "Let's go. Line it up. We got five gassers."

Some of the guys on the team moan and groan about having to run the gassers. Jack and I jog over to the line. We can run all day.

After practice and with pounding headaches, Jack and I leave the locker room anticipating the new depth charts—with a new first-string backfield and two new linebackers. I ride my bike over to the gym to meet Cindy after her cheerleading practice. When I get close to Cindy, I can smell the scent of vanilla. I love being close to her. She grabs her bike, and we head toward her house.

"How was practice?" I ask.

"Really good. We choreographed two new cheers today. How about you?" she asks.

Pedaling next to her, I start to tell her the story. "Jack and I were battling like warriors. It was awesome! You should have seen the looks on the faces of Coach Murphy and Coach Miller."

Cindy swerves from side to side. "I knew you could do it."

I pop a wheelie on the Exploder. "We kicked some butt today." Laughing to myself, I say, "We just about killed each other."

Cindy's green eyes widen. "Look out Unionville! Here comes Billy Morris and Jack Thompson."

CHAPTER 8
August 12

The new depth charts hang from the white cinder block in the locker room. Sliding my finger to the linebacker and running back positions, I find my name and Jack's name. We did it! We earned starting positions on offense and defense for the Unionville varsity football team.

Jack comes up behind me, pushes me on the shoulder, and says, "Way to go, bro! It's me and you."

"The Billy and Jack attack!" I say, raising my hand for a fist bump.

While we dress for practice, John Phillips, Adam Tolliger, Ron Jacobs, and Willy Canter mope around the locker room, and they even shoot Jack and me angry stares. I'm sure they can't believe that they will be second string to two sophomores during their senior year. I don't feel bad for them. They didn't work hard over the summer, and they have to accept the consequences.

Practice includes some hitting, but mostly we focus on running plays against the scout offense and defense. We run our offensive plays over and over until the timing is perfect. It is an honor to be in the first-string huddle with Danny Towers. Even though he's only seventeen years old, he is a natural leader. He commands respect in the huddle, and he runs the team like a finely tuned machine. His drops and steps are perfect. His ball fakes are smooth, like a magician. His arm is a cannon. He hits his receivers on the numbers every time. He throws from a three-step drop, a five-step drop, a rollout right, and a rollout left across his body. Everyone knows how hard he has worked over the summer. This summer he went to three different football camps—Penn State, Notre Dame, and Youngstown State—that focused on the quarterback position. Even I can see that he has improved over the summer, and as a senior, he will probably beat his own records from last year. Danny wants to win Unionville a state championship in the worst way.

Practice flies by today, and I'm completely jacked up about being in the first-string huddle on defense. At one point, Coach Miller pulls me aside and says, "Morris, I want you to be the leader of the defense. Do you think you can call the plays?"

"Yes, sir," I say. "I'm your man." As I think about being the leader of the defense, my heart pounds inside my chest. I do my best to take charge of the defensive huddle. I call the base defense and any stunts by the defensive line or defensive backs. Jack gives two thumbs up to me from his position in the back of the huddle. After we break the huddle, I call the slants and adjustments from my linebacker position.

Everything seems perfect. Everything is going my way. Practice is going great. I have achieved my goal: two starting positions on the varsity football team. I prove to myself that hard work makes anything possible. Because of my dedication over the summer, my dream has become a reality. Along with Jack, I am ready to be a hometown hero and to win Unionville a state championship.

Walking in the front door of my house, I toss my football equipment into the laundry room and smell the pasta sauce on the stove. My mom calls, "Billy, come in the kitchen. There's something we need to talk about."

When I enter the kitchen, my eyes lock on Dick, who is standing directly behind my mom with his left hand on her left shoulder. He is dressed in a powder-blue golf shirt and khaki pants, and he wears a devious grin.

"What's up?" I ask.

Dick remains behind my mother and squeezes her shoulder as she talks. "Billy, honey, you know how I told you I've been thinking about moving?" She pauses and turns her head to look at Dick. "Well, *we've* been thinking about moving."

My heart stops. I try to gain my composure. Here it goes, I think to myself. The topic my mom had brought up earlier in the summer. "I'm not going anywhere," I say.

"We've talked about this before. Richard and I have been thinking about it for a while."

Images of leaving Unionville flash through my mind, all the hard work and my varsity football positions, Jack, and Cindy. It's like being in a horrible dream. My whole world is a giant boulder rolling down a mountain, out of control. "Why now? Why right at the beginning of football season?"

"We wanted to be sure it was something we wanted to do before we told you about the decision," she continues calmly.

I finally find some words. "Football just started. I found out today that I'm going to be the starting varsity linebacker and tailback."

The look on my mom's face changes from certainty to uncertainty, and for a moment, she is silent. "Listen," she gathers herself, "I know how hard you've worked this summer, but Richard ... I need to get out of this town. I need to do something else with my life."

"What about my life?" I shout. Then, all of what she has said hits me. "Wait, what do you mean you and *him?"* I ask, pointing at Dick with one finger and gripping the back of the kitchen chair with my other hand. "He put you up to this."

"This is my decision," says my mom, looking over her shoulder at Dick. "We're sending you to Bertram—you know, where Richard went to boarding school. He says it was the best thing that ever happened to him."

"I'm sure it was the best thing that happened to *him,* but Bertram is not for me. Besides, how are you going to afford Bertram?" I ask.

"They offer financial aid," my mom says, like the answer is obvious.

"What about an entrance exam? I could never get into a school like Bertram."

"Richard has made all the arrangements."

"I'm sure he has." I pause and then say, "Are you guys planning on getting married?"

My mom glances at Dick. "Not right away. We just want to get out of Unionville."

"So, you're ripping my life away from me just so you can be in warmer weather!"

Mom fires back, "Working at that factory is all I do! I want out!"

"Why are you doing this?" I point at Dick. "It's all because of him." I narrow my eyes and clench my fists. Trying to collect myself, I look at my mom and say, "What if I stay here and live with Jack, or maybe I could stay with Cindy's family?"

"No. You are not their responsibility. You're my responsibility." My mom looks at me with resolve in her eyes.

"Your responsibility that you want to ship off to boarding school, just like that!"

"Watch yourself, young man." My mother is usually a pushover, but she doesn't budge this time. I think Dick has coached her. He continues to stand behind her like a coward, holding her in front of him like one of the blocking bags we use in practice.

Feeling hopeless, I say, "There's got to be another way. Everything in my life is here. My friends, football—everything is here!"

"This is in your best interest," my mom retaliates.

"How do *you* know what's in *my* best interest? Unionville is where I belong!"

"Unionville's academics are good, but you'll get a better education at Bertram."

Dick finally speaks. "Bertram is a great school, and I'm sure you know they won the Division II state championship last year. Bertram has great teachers and a top-notch athletic program." The guy sounds like a cheap radio advertisement.

I look at him, and then back at my mother. My mother's eyes indicate that her mind is made up—her decision is final, and nothing will change it. Everything I have worked so hard for has been torn from me.

My mother, trying to comfort me, explains, "Bertram only has a nine-game schedule. Double sessions start this Monday. I already talked to the coach. You won't miss a single practice. You should pack tonight. Tomorrow, we'll drive up to Cleveland and move you into your dorm."

"I am *not* leaving Unionville!" I yell. As I turn toward the stairs to leave the kitchen, I punch the wall with all my might. The plaster gives way, leaving a hole.

My mother shouts, "You get back here right now!"

I storm down the steps to the basement and slam my bedroom door, locking it behind me. I pick up my cell phone and call Jack.

"What up, Billy?" Jack answers.

"Dude, listen to this," I start, and then I give him the rundown of the bomb my mother just dropped.

After a few moments of silence, Jack says, "I would ask my dad if you could come live with us, but he can barely take care of himself, much less me and you. He's already passed out."

"I would never ask you to do that," I say. "What am I going to do? What am I going to tell Coach?"

"I don't understand why your mom is doing it now, without any warning."

"I don't know either. She's been hinting at it all summer. I'm sure Dick has something to do with it. That guy hasn't liked me since day one. All he ever talks about is Bertram Academy and what a star he was."

"When are you supposed to leave?" Jack asks.

"My mom says I'm supposed to pack so we can leave tomorrow. Double sessions start Monday."

"Tomorrow? I wish there was something I could do."

"Yeah, me, too. Listen, I have to call Cindy."

"I'll stop by in the morning."

"Thanks."

I hang up the phone and dial Cindy's cell phone.

"Hey, Billy," she answers in her usual cheerful voice.

"Hey," I say, feeling deflated and defeated.

"What's wrong?"

"Listen to this. My mom and Dick are sending me to Bertram. She said I have to pack tonight, and we're driving there tomorrow." I barely get the words out, and my right hand is throbbing from punching the wall.

"Who is your mom's boyfriend to make those decisions about your life? He's not your father. Isn't there anything I can do? I can ask my dad if you could stay with us."

"My mom said I'm not your family's responsibility and that going to Bertram is in my best interest. Period, end of discussion."

"Are you serious? This can't be happening. Everything was starting to go your way. Our way."

"You're telling me."

"I am so sorry."

"Yeah, me, too. You and Jack, and all my friends, mean everything to me."

"Why is your mom doing this? She isn't even giving you any time to say goodbye. Can I at least come by to see you tomorrow?"

"I was hoping you would."

"I'll be there." On the other end of the line, I can hear Cindy crying.

I hit the "End" button on my cell phone and stare at the ceiling. I think about Cindy, Jack, and playing for Unionville with my best friends. Going to Bertram will mean more than just moving. It will mean leaving friends who are more like brothers. I punch my heavy bag in my room with my already sore hand until my knuckles start to bleed and the tears run down my cheeks. Wiping the tears from my face, I reach down into the angriest part of my soul and promise myself that I'll never cry again.

CHAPTER 9

August 13

On Sunday morning, after a bunch of my friends from the team have already come and gone to say goodbye, Jack shows up. He sits across from me in his sleeveless Unionville football shirt. Just looking at the shirt makes me miss being here already.

"I'll keep you posted on everything that's going on," he says, probably in an attempt to make me feel better.

In Jack's face, I can see his sincerity and appreciate his friendship more than ever. "Thanks a lot, man," I say.

"Hey, you got time for a quick game of PlayStation?" Jack asks.

"Why not?" I say, as I load the college football game.

For forty-five minutes, Jack and I talk about flag football games, tree houses, and all the good times we had growing up in Unionville. We talk about our first day as freshmen, dances, detentions, and summer nights with Cindy and Leigh.

Before he leaves, Jack takes a silver chain off his neck. It has a silver medal on it. One side has a picture of an angel looking over two children. The other side has St. Michael standing on a mountaintop fighting off a dragon. He hands it to me. "Here," he says. "Whenever I get upset, I just hold on to St. Michael. See, he's fighting that dragon."

Shaking my head, I say, "I can't take this from you. It's from your mom."

Jack puts the medal in my hand. "Just don't lose it, okay?"

I take the chain from Jack because I can see that he's sincere, that he wants me to have it. I slip it over my head. "I won't lose it. Thanks."

A knock comes at my bedroom door. Jack says, "I have to get going. Take care of yourself. Don't forget to call me."

We give each other a high five and lean in for a half hug. Jack says hello to Cindy as he walks upstairs. I hear him say goodbye to my mom as he walks out the front door.

Cindy tries to hide her face. Her bright green eyes are bloodshot. "This was supposed to be our year," she says.

"I don't know what to say. This wasn't my decision."

With a hopeful look, Cindy says, "My parents actually said you could stay with us."

I shrug my shoulders. "My mom already said no way to that idea."

Cindy holds my hand. "I don't want you to go."

"I don't want to go either." When I look at Cindy, I begin to realize how much I really care about her. I always knew that I did, but now it seems like I care about her more than ever.

My mom calls from upstairs. "C'mon, Billy. We've got to get going."

I give Cindy a hug. She takes my face in both of her hands and brings her lips to mine, and she kisses me. I didn't know how much emotion could be conveyed with a kiss, but Cindy manages to show me how much she cares about me with that one kiss. I don't want to let go.

At the front door, she looks at me and says, "Call me."

"Of course I will." I walk her to the end of my driveway.

She pulls out an iPod Shuffle. "Here," she says, "I got this for you last night and put a bunch of our favorite songs on it."

Looking down, I say, "I didn't get you anything."

Cindy waves it off. "You had enough going on last night."

"Thanks for everything."

"Just don't forget to call." She wipes the tears from her eyes and gives me a huge hug.

When I walk back into the house, I head down to the basement and call Coach Murphy.

He answers, "Hello?"

"Hi, Coach. It's Billy, Billy Morris."

"What's up, Morris? You okay? You stub your toe or something?"

"Not quite. I've uh, got some bad news." This is harder than I thought. "My mom decided to move to South Carolina, and she's sending me to Bertram Academy."

Coach Murphy is silent on the other end of the line. After what seems like forever, he speaks up. "I hope you understand that your mother is doing what she feels is best for you. Sometimes, decisions like this are beyond our control. I'm real sorry to hear that. We're going to miss you, son. But I want you to know something. I want you to know that I am real proud of how hard you worked this summer. You are one of the hardest workers on this team. That's why the coaches and I decided to go with you and Thompson as starters this year. We wanted hard workers to represent our team. Just remember, wherever you go, you will be successful because of the kind of person you are. You just keep working hard. Whatever you do, don't ever give up. We're sorry to see you go."

Coach Murphy's words make me feel proud, but at the same time, I feel like I'm letting down the entire town. "Coach, I'm sorry for letting you down."

"Billy, this isn't your fault. Make the best of the situations that life throws at you. I have some news for you. Life isn't always good and easy. There are going to be lots of obstacles. You have to face that stuff head-on."

I am filled with regret because I will not be playing for Coach Murphy or Coach Miller. "Coach, thanks for everything. I'll make you proud at Bertram."

"Good luck, son."

I say goodbye and hang up the phone.

My mom, now clearly annoyed, says, "Billy, let's go. Put your stuff in the car. We need to get going."

Unfortunately, when I make it upstairs, I see that Dick is going to Cleveland with us. I completely ignore Dick, and my mother gives me an angry look. I load two large suitcases and a backpack into the trunk of our silver Buick.

We drive north. After five freeways and four hours of complete silence, we pull up to the entrance of the school, where large, cast-iron gates greet us. We pass open fields, tennis courts, and large brick buildings. The long winding driveway is lined with leafy giant maple and oak trees. It eventually leads to the red-brick, ivy-covered admissions office.

Dick breaks the silence when he says, "Ah yes, the old stomping grounds. Got some great memories from my time here at Bertram. I remember my senior year, had twenty-two tackles in one game. Got my name on a plaque on the Wall of Fame."

Sitting in the back seat, I am silent, still feeling betrayed.

Coach Murphy's words echo in my mind. *Make the best of the situation. Life is full of unexpected obstacles. You need to face them head-on.*

My mother interrupts my thoughts. "Look, there are some of the football players. They must be here for double sessions." As she utters these words, we turn the corner. A sign posted on the gate reads: Football Check-in and Student Registration. My mother parks the car in a lot that is half full. I expect to see Mercedes and Porsches, but I am surprised to see nice cars and a few beaters.

In the gym, forty or so guys are registering for their rooms and receiving their itineraries for practice. I stand in line next to a boy whom I recognize. He has brown hair, brown eyes, and his gray T-shirt with cut-off sleeves exposes his well-defined biceps. I remember playing against him as a freshman at Unionville.

The kid recognizes me and says, "Hey, aren't you Billy Morris?"

Nodding my head, I say, "Yeah, that's me."

He reaches out his hand. "I'm Kevin, Kevin Gordon. I played against you last year. I played for Iron City."

"I remember you. You're one of the toughest hitters we faced all year."

Kevin's face lights up with the compliment, and he says, "You guys were the best team we played all year. We couldn't stop you and your fullback. What's his name?"

"Jack Thompson," I answer, feeling proud but sad to say his name.

"Yeah, Thompson, that's it." Kevin shakes his head and smiles. "Man, that dude was tough."

Kevin and I start talking like old friends. Last year we were bitter rivals, but our common situation brings us together almost immediately. Kevin and I get our room assignments. I am in room 42, on the fourth floor. Kevin's room assignment is the same. Kevin seems to be as happy as I am. At least we won't be rooming with total strangers. We look over our itineraries. There is a meeting tonight with the football team, and then I start double sessions all over again. Tomorrow, I will have to prove myself to a whole new set of coaches and a whole new team.

Looking around the room, I notice that a lot of the athletes at Bertram are good-sized kids. Most are returning after a year when they won the Division II state championship. I followed their season in articles from the newspaper. The school has a bunch of players returning for their senior year, so it won't be easy to earn a spot on this team. Terrance Strong, a returning starter from the year before, already fills the tailback position. Last year, he was All-State as a junior. I figure he will be one of the people I will be competing with for the position of tailback. I'm not sure who the linebackers are, but I'm sure that my work will be cut out for me. I do have one advantage. I have already gone through the soreness of my first week of double sessions, and I feel strong.

Kevin and I check into our room on the fourth floor. Dick and my mother help me carry my things to my room. There is no elevator, so for once in my life, I am glad that Dick is with us.

Kevin says, "I forgot one of my bags downstairs. I'll be back in a minute."

When Kevin leaves, my mother asks, "So, what do you think?"

"Does it matter?" I look around my new room, which contains two desks, two closets, and two beds.

"I think this is a great place, a great opportunity." My mom places my backpack on the floor, and Dick puts one of my suitcases on the bed.

"If you say so," I reply in a sarcastic tone.

"You're going to be fine." My mom starts to unpack my suitcase, placing some T-shirts in the top dresser drawer.

"Whatever you say."

She hangs some dress shirts in the closet, and then she pulls out some sheets and starts to put them on the bed. As she slides my pillow into a pillowcase, she says, "I really think this is going to be a good thing for you."

"Mom, I think this," I open my arms, gesturing toward the room, "is something that's going to be good for *you*, not me."

She takes a deep breath, probably considering whether now is a good time to get into it. Choosing to avoid a confrontation, she merely says, "We have a long ride back to Unionville, so we'll let you settle in." She gives me a hug. "I love you."

I feel a surge of panic, and my heart starts to pound. I have never lived on my own before, and the thought of being on my own scares me to death. I can barely keep myself together. But when I start to say something, I stop myself, remembering that I promised myself I wouldn't show any emotions, so I don't.

In my mother's face is a sense of uncertainty; maybe she's having second thoughts about her decision.

She hugs me again and says, "Study hard, keep up the good work on the football field, eat well, and call me. I'll miss you."

I don't even bother to say goodbye to Dick, who I'm sure is already celebrating the fact that he doesn't have to deal with me anymore.

Dick leaves my room first, and my mom closes the door behind her.

I begin to unpack the rest of my things. From my fourth story window, I see my mom and Dick walking across the parking lot and climbing into the silver Buick. I watch as the car snakes down the winding road from the academy.

Kevin opens the door and walks back in the room and says, "Team meeting is in thirty minutes." He smiles and says, "It's go time."

I manage a fake smile.

Kevin unpacks his things as he tells me his story, which is much different from mine. "Man, I am just glad to be here. This is an opportunity of a lifetime. Things in Iron City weren't looking too good. You know, we haven't had a good team in a while."

When we played against Kevin, our team dominated the game. Kevin was one of the only kids who could actually play. The school's varsity team wasn't much better and hadn't won more than five games in a season over the last five years.

Kevin says, "I want to play for a winner. My dad pulled some strings to get me into Bertram. Plus, Bertram gives me the best chance to get into a good college."

I tell Kevin my story about how my mom and Dick turned my life inside out.

With a look of complete shock, Kevin says, "You gave up two varsity positions as a sophomore? Man, that is a raw deal."

"Yeah, well, I guess I gotta make the best of it," I say, sitting down on my bed.

Kevin continues to unpack his things. "It's weird. I'm excited to be here, and you wish you didn't have to be."

"I guess it's all how you see it."

"Yeah, I guess so." He throws some jeans into an empty drawer.

"So, I guess that meeting starts in about ten minutes?"

Kevin finishes unpacking the rest of his clothes and says, "Yeah, we'd better get going."

In the auditorium at the school, we have our first meeting with the coaches of Bertram Academy. Metal chairs are lined up in front of a stage with a podium. The head coach walks past the podium, gets down from the stage, and stands in front of his team. The coach is not as big as Coach Murphy, but I can tell that he commands respect. He doesn't laugh or joke around. His salt-and-pepper hair is neatly combed, and his red-and-black collared shirt is neatly tucked into his black shorts. When he faces the team, there is complete silence.

"Welcome everybody. I am Coach Carlson. These are my assistants: Linebacker Coach and Defensive Coordinator, Coach Kaplan; Defensive Back and Wide Receiver Coach, Coach Stevens; and Offensive and Defensive Line Coach, Coach Benjamin. I will be coaching the running backs and quarterbacks as well as calling the plays. Coach Kaplan will be calling the defense. As I look around, I see some old faces and some new faces.

We had an unbelievable season last year, winning the Division II state championship. With the returning starters from last year, I believe we should be able to repeat that accomplishment this year. Hopefully, all of you put in the necessary work this summer to achieve that goal." He looks around at all the players and gives a little smile. "Well, we'll figure that out soon enough once practice starts tomorrow. I'm proud to say that we have some new players joining us this year. My advice to you new players: don't sit back and let other people take charge. Even though we have a lot of returning starters, that doesn't mean the positions will be handed to them this year. All positions will be earned. Also, for all new players, I will go over the dorm rules." A groan comes from all the players. "There is a nine o'clock curfew, and lights are out at ten. Don't try me on these rules. If you are out past curfew, you will be written up. Three write-ups, and you will be on probation, which means no football. Is that clear?"

"Yes, Coach," the team replies in unison.

"And finally," Coach Carlson adds, "our first double session starts tomorrow at 8:00 a.m. Don't be late. If you can't be on time, be on Coach Carlson time, and that's ten minutes early. I expect great things from this team. Tonight, look over and learn the first ten pages of the offensive playbook and the first ten pages of your defensive playbook. Pay particular attention to your position and what you are supposed to do on each play. Also, pay attention to what all the other positions are doing so you can understand the scheme of our offense and defense.

Come prepared tomorrow. The first three days will be without pads. The fourth day will be with pads, and on the fifth day, we start hitting."

With that announcement, all the players, except for me, whoop and yell at the anticipation of the first day of hitting. Coach Carlson finishes, "Men, seniors especially, this is your team. Make this year special."

That night, Kevin and I go over our playbooks together. Bertram runs a similar offense and defense to Unionville. Kevin struggles a little bit. I explain the new formations to him, and he starts to pick things up.

When we finish, Kevin turns out the light and gets into his bed on the opposite side of the room. I walk over to the fourth-story window, slide it open, and look outside. A cool breeze floats in the window. I scan the lit-up campus and look up at the stars that illuminate the night sky. I power on the iPod that Cindy gave me. As I listen to the first song on Cindy's playlist, I consider the events that took place over the last twenty-four hours and have a hard time believing that this is my new reality. Looking down on the old brick buildings and the large campus that make up my new home, I can only hope that I will survive at Bertram Academy.

CHAPTER 10
August 14

I wake up to unfamiliar surroundings and a cool morning breeze. Kevin is snoring in the bed on the other side of the dorm room. My nightmare from yesterday has become my reality. I'm really here, at Bertram Academy. I want someone to pinch me and wake me up, tell me it's all been a mistake. As I stare at a few cracks on the ceiling, I think about Jack and the guys from Unionville—how they will be practicing today, how their lives will go on like normal. My positions will be filled. My name will be erased from the depth chart in the coach's office, just like that, with one swipe of the eraser. In the middle of thinking about Unionville, it occurs to me that I forgot to call Cindy last night. I go to grab my phone before I realize she is probably on her way to cheerleading practice.

Kevin stirs in his bed and rolls over. In a groggy, early-morning voice, he says, "Hey, man. What's up?"

"I just can't believe this. I already did my first week of double sessions."

Kevin sits up, resting on his elbows. "Just think, you're one step ahead of the game. You're already in good shape. This week will be easy for you."

"I guess we'll find out," I mumble.

Kevin is a fullback and linebacker, so we will be in competition with each other for the starting linebacker position. It's one of the only positions on defense that needs to be filled. Almost the entire defense is returning from last year. It is rare for a group of juniors to win a state championship.

The field house is walking distance from the football field. Kevin and I jog down the gravel road past the freshly cut field hockey and lacrosse fields on our left. Off in the distance are two baseball diamonds on the left and two soccer fields on the right. At the end of the gravel road is the football stadium with red-painted bleachers. A huge eagle sculpture sits at the entrance to the stadium. The sign over the entrance reads: Bertram Eagles: Division II State Champions. As I walk past the eagle, chills shoot through my body. At the field house, we pull out our play-books, and Coach Carlson addresses the team. "Men," he begins, "these will be the running plays we will put in today. I cannot stress enough the importance of timing and teamwork. Each person needs to know everyone's job." I wonder if all head coaches give the same speech on the first day of double sessions.

Out on the field, we begin running through our offensive groups. I'm in the tailback group with Terrance Strong. He's a stud, not that big, about six feet, but he can fly. He glides on the field effortlessly. The football field is his natural habitat, like he was born there.

During a break, I ask Kevin, "How did Terrance end up at Bertram?"

"He transferred his freshman year from a school down in Columbus, didn't play much as a freshman or as a sophomore, but last year he was the starting tailback. He's got like 4.5 speed. It looks like he got even faster over the summer. Did you see him run those plays? Man, he's fast."

"Yeah, you can say that again. The guy is like a freak of nature." The sun beats down and the humidity rises as we start our offensive session in the afternoon. I run with the third group of backs, which isn't very impressive because there are only three groups. Bertram does not have many players, only fifty-five guys all together. My new job is to get water from the trainer for the starting offense and defense. In a matter of two days, I've gone from first-string-varsity to third-string-water-boy, but I refuse to feel sorry for myself.

I run each drill at full speed. The week of practice with Unionville makes my first practice at Bertram more bearable. Even though our third-string quarterback is just learning the plays, I help him and Kevin out. Kevin plays fullback with my group. The only advantage of being in the third group is that we have the opportunity to see the play run twice before we actually have to do it. We work well together. Kevin has good speed and always manages to get out of the way of the pitches on sweeps, and he hits the holes hard.

Between plays, I say to Kevin, "I think we can move up to second string when the hitting drills start. The two juniors are not that strong. The only thing they have on us is that they ran the same offense last year. Terrance and Sammy, on the other hand, look like they should be in the freaking NFL."

Terrance Strong stands deep in the I-formation and explodes from his stance, faster than anybody I have ever seen. The fullback, Sammy Jones, is just as awesome. Sammy and Terrance move like one person, anticipating each other's moves.

There's a better chance to start on defense. The team has only four linebackers, and Kevin and I are two of them. One of them is a junior, Joey Tate, who looks to be a decent athlete. The other linebacker is Marcus Tyler. At five foot eight inches tall and 225 pounds, he is like a human bowling ball.

The linebacker coach, Coach Kaplan, puts Marcus and Joey as the starters. I run in the second group with Kevin. Coach Kaplan says, "For those of you who don't know, I played ball at the University of Michigan. If you boys dedicate yourselves and work hard, one day, you can play Division I ball. The groups you've been placed in are for learning the base defense. Pay attention and learn your reads."

I run the drills with the knowledge I received from Coach Miller. After watching the other players go through the drills, I know that I have a shot at starting at linebacker.

After our individual defensive drills, Coach Kaplan pulls me aside. "Mr. Morris," he says, "who taught you how to play linebacker?"

"My coach at Unionville," I utter proudly. "He played middle linebacker at Ohio State."

"Ohio State, huh?" He shakes his head and smiles. "Well, even though you learned your skills from a Buckeye, your steps are good, your pursuit is downhill, and you make no false steps. You do a nice job reading the guards, and your pass drops are solid." He slaps me on the helmet. "If you can hit, we might just have a spot for you on varsity."

I smile proudly as I walk away. The first day of doubles at Bertram is not as demanding physically compared to Unionville, but being the new kid at the new school is anything but easy. The only person I feel comfortable around is Kevin, and he is my competition for starting at linebacker. I feel like I'm on an island all by myself. On the way back to the dorm, Cindy and Jack are on my mind. I wonder how Cindy is doing with cheerleading, and I want to talk to Jack to see who Coach Murphy replaced me with. Adam Tolliger will probably get to start at tailback, even though he didn't do anything over the summer. Willy Canter will probably be the starting linebacker with Jack.

Suddenly, my stomach starts to turn as I realize that I have been so caught up in leaving my house, moving into my new dorm, and trying to earn a spot on my new team, that I forgot about what I left behind. I think about playing under the lights in Unionville with the entire town watching. I can almost hear the loudspeaker blaring Jack's name and then my name: *Starting at fullback for the Unionville Rockets, sophomore Jack Thompson, and starting at tailback for the Unionville Rockets, sophomore Billy Morris.* I picture the scene in my head: the blue and gold colors scattered throughout the stands, Cindy cheering with a flying Rocket surrounded by little yellow stars painted on each cheek, the band playing and drums pounding as we sprint onto the field—a dream come true.

That evening, I grab my cell phone and walk out onto the campus and call Cindy. The phone rings four or five times until she answers.

"Hello," Cindy answers, sounding annoyed.

"Hey."

"Hey, Billy." There is a long pause, and then Cindy says in an irritated voice, "Why haven't you called? Are you okay? I've been worried about you."

I try to answer the flurry of questions one at a time. "Well, let's see. I've been driving with my mother and Dick, checking into my dorm, and trying to make it through doubles at a new school where I barely know anyone. And to top it off, I miss you, Jack, and everyone else. I haven't had a minute to call, and when I finally thought about it, it was too late."

Cindy backs off. "I've been worried. I haven't stopped thinking about you. I feel like it's all been some horrible dream."

"I know. None of it seems real, and we still have two weeks of practice before school starts."

"So, what's the school like?" Cindy asks.

"It's all right I guess. It's a prep school, but the only thing I'm prepared to do is get out of here."

"You're going to be fine," Cindy says, trying to reassure me. "If anybody can do this, it's you. Those guys are lucky to have you."

"Thanks. That means a lot." Even though Cindy's voice makes me feel better, it also makes me miss her even more.

"Are you doing okay?" she asks.

"I guess I'm doing fine, but we do have a curfew."

"A curfew? Seriously, what time?"

"Lights out at ten."

"That's early."

"I know. I want to talk some more, but I should go. I want to call Jack before lights out. I told him I would."

"I understand, but promise me you'll call."

"I promise. I'll call you tomorrow." I hang up the phone and then call Jack. The phone rings three or four times.

"What up, Billy?"

"What's up, bro?"

"I was hoping you'd call. How's it goin'?" Jack asks.

"Just trying to get through this nightmare."

"Nightmare, huh? How's football going?"

"Dude, the competition is tough. Most of the guys are starters from last year's state championship team."

"You got a chance to start?" Jack asks.

"The tailback position looks pretty locked up. You remember Terrance Strong? That guy is just plain fast. I don't think I have a shot there, but I think there's a spot on the defense at linebacker. If I get it, I'll be the only sophomore starter."

"Good for you, man. Do it. We all miss you. I talked to Cindy after practice yesterday. She's super bummed about you leaving. I told her you guys would keep in touch, and everything would be okay."

"Thanks, man. I appreciate it. I've been worried about her. Hell, I've been worried about me."

"You'll be fine; just keep at it."

"I wish I felt that way. I'm still so pissed at my mom and Dick."

"There's a For Sale sign in your front yard—looks like they're serious about leaving."

"I try not to think about it." To change the subject I ask, "By the way, how's the football team doing?"

"It's good. Coach Miller named me the defensive captain. I couldn't believe it. After you left, I started running the defensive huddle and calling all the plays. He said I was born to be a linebacker. I got all fired up, wanted to lay somebody out. I can't wait for our first scrimmage this weekend, and then we only have two more weeks until our first game."

"That's cool," is all I can get out. Hearing about all the good things happening to Jack in Unionville is hard. And even though he's my best friend, I can't help but feel jealous. He's the captain of the defense; that was supposed to be my job. "Listen, man. I have to run. Lights go out at ten. Good job being named captain."

Jack must notice the tone hidden in my voice. After a long silence, Jack says, "Billy, you're like a brother to me. You're going to be okay. Show those prep-school boys how we do it at Unionville. You'll be the starting linebacker, kicking some ass. You know those guys don't have what you got. You worked too hard this summer to let them take what's yours."

"You know, you're right." Jack's words lift my spirit.

"Let me know how the hitting goes. I want to know if those Bertram boys have any courage."

"You got it, man! I'm going to show 'em what Unionville football is all about. You're a real friend."

"You better light somebody up for me."

"You got it, bro. I'll call you later."

"Later."

CHAPTER 11
August 18–23

Over the next two days, we put in play after play on offense and overload our playbooks with defensive schemes. Coach Carlson stresses the strategic part of the game more than Coach Murphy. Coach Carlson has great players, but not much depth. He puts the right players in the right positions. He moves players around, giving them new positions as the days go by. There is not one selfish player on the team. When players are asked to move to new positions, they just do it without question. I guess they figure it's in the best interest of the team, and in a short period of time, those players excel at their new positions. Coach Carlson understands personnel in the game of football. With a limited number of players, he created a Division II powerhouse. Of course, it doesn't hurt when All-State tailback Terrance Strong is in your backfield.

On our fourth day of practice, acclimation day, Terrance and I have our first run in. Because I am a second-string linebacker, I play on the scout defense. Our job is to give the first offense a good look, while they blast into us to perfect their blocking schemes. If we do get a shot at the running back, we are only supposed to give them a good fit, wrap them up.

Coach Carlson calls the plays on the offensive side of the ball. The offense is smooth. Ten of the eleven players, except for the quarterback, Mike Giffin, are seniors and returning starters from the state championship team. Their flawless execution shows why they won state. Because Terrance and I have not yet been introduced, I'm just the new sophomore, a nobody. On a dive play, he runs through the line of scrimmage. My offensive lineman misses his block, and I am one on one with Terrance. When I go to wrap him up, he makes a quick move and jukes to the outside. Because we are not going full go, my timing is off, and I miss the tackle, falling flat on my face. I can hear Terrance laugh at me as he runs toward the end zone. On his way back to the huddle, he throws the ball, and it hits me in the back of the helmet. Instantly, I flip my switch to full go.

Terrance has pissed off the wrong guy.

I ask Coach Kaplan, who runs the scout defense, "Can we go full go?"

He shakes his head. "Don't worry about it. Practice is for the offensive team. They need to get a good look."

Jack's words ring in my ears. *Show those prep-school boys how we do it.*

Before the next play, I decide that enough is enough. I line up over the guard in our 52 defense. The guard pulls, and I read sweep. I take my course toward the running back. Making no false steps, my course is downhill toward the line of scrimmage. My technique is perfect. Avoiding the blocking from the inside, I maneuver behind the pulling guard. Playing inside out like I was taught at Unionville, I shoot through the gap and meet Terrance head-on in the hole, place my facemask on the ball, and execute a perfect form tackle. There is a loud pop. I wrap his legs with my arms and pull them to my chest. Terrance grunts as I lift him off his feet during the violent collision and drive him into the ground. I step on his hand and push off on his facemask to stand up. I glare down at him and tell him, "Stay down."

In an instant, Terrance is up on his feet and in my face. Coaches and teammates come running and try to get between us. The offense is pushing and shoving, and, to my surprise, the scout defense has my back, led by Kevin Gordon. Bodies are flying everywhere.

Terrance is in the thick of the mob, shouting every swear word he knows and yelling, *"I'm gonna kill you, next chance I get!"*

I point my finger at Terrance and yell back, *"You're not good enough to be running your mouth!"*

"I'm gonna tear you apart," Terrance threatens.

"I'm right here! Not afraid of you," I shout back.

The pushing and shoving continues for what seems like an eternity. Coach Carlson finally blows his whistle as loudly as he can four or five times in a row until the two groups quiet down and are separated by the coaches. Each group is standing shoulder to shoulder, unwilling to give any ground. The scout defense has made a stand. Maybe we are just sophomores, but we are also members of the team and deserve that respect. I'm sure Coach Carlson isn't too thrilled that I just stuck his All-State tailback, but I hope he feels like he found someone who is fearless and loves to play the game the way it should be played. One more spot is still available on the starting defense at linebacker, and nobody wants it more than I do.

After we hit the showers, I make my way back to my dorm on campus. Out of the corner of my eye I see Terrance coming right at me. I stand my ground, expecting a right hook. Instead, he walks up to me and extends his hand. I give him a funny look, and he shakes his head and says, "Friends?"

"You and me?" I ask.

"We're a team. Coach sat me down and said I had it coming. Said you put me in my place, and that might've been a good thing."

"No worries." I reach out my hand to shake his.

"Are we cool, Morris?"

"Yeah, we're cool."

So that is that. A little controversy has earned me some respect, a lesson that I will not forget. *No matter what, stand up for yourself.*

The next day is a full-go, hit day. I'm up before the alarm goes off, staring at the wall and my Ray Lewis poster. Just looking at the poster gets me fired up.

Kevin wakes up with the alarm. He rubs his eyes and sits up in his bed. He looks at me and sees that I've been up for a while. "What's up, man?" he asks.

"Can't sleep. Not on days like this."

Kevin puts his feet on the white floor tiles and says groggily, "Hey, man. Time to earn a position. You think coach will put you against Terrance after yesterday?"

"I doubt it. The farther away I am from Terrance, the better."

Kevin and I are in competition for the starting line-backer spot. When hit day comes around, I put myself in a different world. I go into the zone, a place where things are nasty and intense. I have no friends on hit day. It isn't about friendship; it's about football, survival, and courage. If you don't approach it that way, then you usually spend most of your time on the bench as a spectator. I am not a good spectator.

It is my second hit day with my second team in only two weeks, but I'm proud of the way I'm handling being the new kid at the new school. It isn't easy.

Coach Carlson starts practice by saying, "Men, today is the day you've been waiting for. Today is a chance to earn a position. We have each player partnered up. After that, you can jump in as many drills as you can."

We head out for stretching and warm-up laps. After our warm-up, we are put into our hitting groups. Joey Tate is my partner. Joey is a good athlete, but hitting is not his strong point. On the first drill, I run him over, making him wish he were a wide receiver. He walks out of the drill with his head down.

In the next drill, I am up against Kevin. I remember from last year that he is a tough kid, but he will be no match for me today. The drills with Kevin are intense. In one, Kevin is the ball carrier, and I'm the defender. It is a pursuit drill that brings us into a head-on collision. I take a good course and lower my shoulder. I wrap up Kevin and drive him four yards out of bounds.

Kevin jumps to his feet and slaps me on the helmet and says, "Good hit." Kevin is too nice.

In between sessions, Coach Kaplan pulls me aside. "Billy, you think you're ready to start on the varsity?"

I look Coach Kaplan in the eye and say, "It's all I want."

He pats me on the back and says, "Good, you'll be starting at linebacker with Marcus."

I nod my head and feel energized. I can't wait to tell Jack.

After practice, Kevin says, "Coach Kaplan told me I did a good job today. He said I'd be second-string line-backer and share time at nose guard. What did he tell you?"

"I'll be starting at linebacker with Marcus—not to let him down."

Kevin slaps me on the shoulder pads. "Congratulations, man. Way to go."

Kevin is not only a good athlete, but he's becoming a good friend. At the afternoon practice, I take my spot in the defensive huddle as the weak-side linebacker, the scrape-backer. Marcus is the fill-backer. His job is to fill the holes; my job is to scrape along the defensive line and punish the ball carrier. I'm glad that I was at Unionville for the first week of practice. Coach Miller taught me more than technique. He taught me about attitude, that believing you can do something is just as important as doing it. I learned to stand up for myself and gained the confidence to earn the starting linebacker position at Bertram.

After practice on Saturday, I realize that summer weekends are dead at Bertram. I try calling Cindy, but she doesn't answer. I call Jack's phone, but it goes directly to his voicemail. On my bed, even though I'm only four hours from Unionville, I feel like I'm a million miles away.

Kevin lumbers into the room, checks his spiky hair in the mirror and says, "Hey, man. What's up?"

"Not much, trying to get a hold of some of my friends back home."

"Feeling homesick?" Kevin asks.

Looking down, I say, "Yeah, I guess you could say that. I miss Cindy and Jack. Jack and I are like brothers.

So many of my friends from Unionville I've known since first grade. It's hard to think about not being in their lives anymore."

Kevin nods. "Yeah, I totally understand. I had a bunch of good friends back home, but there was no future there. The school would never give me the opportunities I'll have here. I never had any homework. I want to go to a good college, and Bertram gives me the best chance to do that."

"School has never been at the top of my list."

"Well, you'd better put school at the top of your list. From what I hear, Bertram is tough."

Kevin and I end up sitting up until two in the morning talking about school, friends, and sports. Turns out, we have a ton of things in common. I tell Kevin about Jack and Cindy, and he tells me about his girlfriend. He's already received a few letters from her. She always signs them: Love, Denise, and she sprays them with her perfume.

Kevin turns out the light, and soon, he's fast asleep. But I can't sleep. In my mind, I can't help but think about Cindy and Jack. I miss Tombo and Woody. Thinking back to my last day of school at Unionville and the car ride with Leigh after my workout, I remember her words: *The whole world is based on timing.* I can't help but think about what could have been if I had stayed in Unionville, and how different my life is now that I'm at Bertram. Terrance and Kevin and the coaches at Bertram have already been a huge influence on my life—who will be next?

CHAPTER 12

August 24

It's Sunday morning, and we have the day off. I'm up early, but Kevin is still sleeping. Because I don't want to bother him, I quietly get up, get dressed, and walk toward the cafeteria for breakfast. Strolling through the center of campus, I notice a sign posted on the gymnasium door that reads: Field Hockey Registration.

Finally, I think, *girls*. The one good thing about Bertram is that it's co-ed. Some of the private schools around here are either all-boys or all-girls. Thank God I won't be surrounded by a bunch of guys all the time.

On the way to the cafeteria, I can smell the bacon and eggs outside the door. After filling my plate, I sit in the corner of the dining hall and look through the giant picture window with a view of the campus. Eating in silence, I take in the trees and what seems like miles of green grass. I'm the only one here, except for the ladies serving breakfast.

On my way back to my dorm, I lock eyes with a girl. She has brown hair and a dark tan. She holds a bag in one hand and a field hockey stick in the other. I can't stop staring at her, and I'm amazed when she walks right up to me and asks, "Hey, do you know where field hockey registration is?"

"They are … uh, um … in the … uh … gym."

She smiles, showing her perfect teeth. "I know they're in the gym, but where's the gym?"

"Oh," I laugh. "I can take you there. It's just around the corner." Putting my hand out, I say, "By the way, my name is Billy, Billy Morris."

"Nice to meet you, Billy." She puts her stick in her other hand that holds the bag, and she shakes my hand. "I'm Taylor Parker." She looks me up and down. "So, what are you doing here so early before school starts?"

"Football. We started last week. It's been quiet around here. It's good to see some new faces. What about you?"

"Transferred from my old school down in Columbus— Granville High, near Denison."

"I've heard of Denison. Some guys I know went there to play ball." I'm such an idiot. Is football the only thing I can talk about? "So this is your first year here, like me?"

"Yeah, but I think I already said that," Taylor says.

"Right, you did." I want to punch myself in the head.

Taylor pushes my shoulder. "I'm just teasing you."

I don't know what comes over me because I'm shy as hell around girls, but I find some courage. "Hey," I mumble, "maybe we could get something to eat later or something?"

"Are you asking me out?" Taylor asks, tilting her head to the side.

I hold my hands up like I'm stopping traffic. "Um, just as friends. You know, two new students."

Taylor looks down for a moment. "Yeah, that sounds nice. Where's your dorm?"

"I'm staying at Stuart Hall. It's on the south side of campus. How about I meet you at the gym at six, tomorrow after practice? Dinner's at 6:30."

"It's a deal."

We arrive at the gym, and I point Taylor in the direction of the registration. She thanks me and goes inside.

On the way back to the dorm, I can't stop thinking about Taylor. I think about that first moment when I saw her. About how she moves. How she smiles with her perfect teeth and perfect lips. How she smells, making me dizzy. Her tanned legs, strong and athletic. I can't stop thinking about how beautiful she is. Did I just say beautiful? I never talk like that. I usually say: "cute," "hot," or "smokin'." I've never seen anyone like her.

And then, out of nowhere, Cindy pops into my mind. Kevin and I talked so late last night that I forgot to call her. She's going to be pissed. Taking my phone out of my bag, I call Cindy.

Cindy answers her phone, but our conversation is brief. It's obvious that she's mad at me because all her answers are short, and I can hear the impatience in her voice. We talk about school starting soon, football, and cheerleading. I do my best to focus on what Cindy is saying, but during the entire conversation, I can't stop thinking about Taylor.

Monday begins our second week of double sessions. We're preparing for a scrimmage at the end of the week. Our first game is on Friday after the first week of school. Bertram plays all home games on Saturday afternoon, a tradition that will take some getting used to. As a freshman at Unionville, I dreamed about playing under the lights on Friday night. At least our away games will be played on Friday nights, but I'm disappointed that our home games won't.

Practice is tough in the humid Ohio heat. The thermometer on the side of the field house reads ninety degrees, and the humidity is unbearable. It's the kind of heat that stops you in your tracks, and the humidity is so heavy it feels like you can swim through it. I run in the second group on offense, and I start to feel more comfortable with my starting position at linebacker, learning all the stunts and the defensive calls. The senior leadership keeps everyone in line. Even though I miss my friends from Unionville, I can't help but think that Bertram Academy has a chance to be state champions again this year.

After practice, I head back to the dorm at 3:30. After I wake up from a solid nap, I jump out of bed and run to the shower to get ready for my dinner with Taylor. I don't want to smell bad. After I shave off a few strands of facial hair, I put on some aftershave and dash out the door at six.

I see Taylor standing under the willow tree in the center of campus, and suddenly everything starts to move in slow motion. The wind picks up and blows across the campus. Her hair flies back, just like in the movies. She looks awesome, better than I remember from yesterday. I have to catch my breath.

"Hey," she says, jumping toward me.

"What's up?" I say, trying to play it cool.

"Not much. We just finished practice. I'm hungry. Come on. Let's eat."

We walk toward the cafeteria in awkward silence. I open the door for her, and we join the food line. Everything smells really good. We make small talk as we move through the line to get our food. I load my plate with mashed potatoes and roast beef, and Taylor makes a salad. We find a table in the back of the cafeteria.

Taylor asks, "How was practice today?"

"Things are okay. This is actually my third week of practice. I already have a week under my belt from my old school."

"Where did you go to school before?"

"Unionville, just east of Dayton." I take a big bite of mashed potatoes.

"So what brings you to Bertram?" she asks.

I scratch my head, knowing the story is complicated. "Well, you see, my mom and her boyfriend decided to move. They weren't sure what to do with me. So here I am."

"Makes you feel important, huh?" Taylor says, and then takes a sip of her Diet Coke.

"Yeah, it pretty much sucks. I earned two spots on the varsity team with my best friend, Jack. This was going to be our year." I catch myself because I'm rambling. Trying to slow down, I say, "Enough about me. How did you end up at Bertram?"

"Well," she begins, "Bertram is a great school. Plus, I play field hockey, and I play the violin. Bertram has one of the best music programs around."

"That's cool. How long have you been playing?" I ask, trying to focus more on her and less on my food.

"Since I was like five. My mom thought it was a good idea for me to learn an instrument. I picked it up pretty fast," she says, looking down at her salad.

"That's nothing to be ashamed of. You should be proud."

She looks up. "You think so?"

Nodding my head, I say, "Definitely. I can't play anything. I admire anyone who can play an instrument. My mom made me take piano lessons for two years, but I was horrible. I could never get my right hand and my left hand to work at the same time."

"The piano is hard to play." Taylor gives me a sheepish smile.

"Yeah, but instead of going to lessons, I used to ride my dirt bike on the trails in the woods behind my house.

It worked until my teacher called my mom and asked her why I hadn't been to lessons in two weeks. My mom told her she thought I was going, so I was big-time busted. I guess my mom figured if I was that unhappy about going to lessons, I shouldn't have to do it. She was actually pretty cool about it."

Taylor laughs at my story, and I can't help but notice her carefree smile. For an instant, I think about Cindy.

Taylor must be able to tell my mind is on something else because she asks, "Penny for your thoughts?"

"I was just thinking about my girlfriend back home."

"Oh, you're seeing someone? How long have you guys been going out?" Taylor asks, sounding disappointed.

"We've been hanging out for about six months, but we've known each other since elementary school. What about you? Are you seeing anybody?"

"It seems like I don't have a lot of time for boyfriends, with sports and the violin and all. Plus, I was in the school play."

"You act, too?" I ask, with some disbelief.

"Yeah, I love it. One of my friends suggested we try out for the spring musical together. The play was *Fiddler on the Roof*. Apparently the matchmaker didn't make me a match." She smiles at this.

I smile back, pretending to know what she's talking about.

"Yeah, so what about you and your girl?" Taylor asks, moving her salad around her plate.

"Well, we promised to keep in touch. I imagine we'll both be busy. She's a cheerleader, and that takes up a lot of her time. I know it'll be harder once school starts."

Taylor nods her head like she gets it. "Well, if she means enough to you, you'll find a way. If it's meant to be, it'll be."

"Yeah, I guess you're right. It's just hard being away from home. I miss my friends. I feel like everything I worked for was for nothing."

Taylor looks me in the eye. "You know, life is weird that way, but I bet you'll find that you're here for a reason. You don't know what that reason is, yet. It's like the forces of the universe, stuff we're not supposed to understand. I'm here because I want to go to Juilliard and eventually play first chair for the New York Symphony. I figure Bertram gives me the best opportunity to do that. I feel lucky to be here."

I let what Taylor says sink in. "I never really looked at it that way. I've been so busy being pissed at my mom for sending me here, I never thought about the opportunities that might be here. I've never been a good student. Never even opened a book at Unionville."

"I can promise you that you'll have plenty of reading to do here," Taylor says.

Taylor and I talk for two hours, and it seems like ten minutes. And once we get started, there is not a moment of awkward silence. She makes me feel comfortable, but all the talk about school is making me nervous. Being so focused on football, I haven't even thought about school. I look at Taylor. In fact, I can't stop looking at her. "I had a great time. Maybe we could hang out again some time?" I shyly suggest.

Taylor glances at me with her dark brown eyes. "Yeah, that sounds cool. This week is busy. I have a team meeting tomorrow night, and Wednesday I have a scrimmage. Thursday might be good."

"Thursday's good for me, too. I have a scrimmage Friday night."

"Thursday it is."

We get up from our table, and I walk Taylor back to her dorm. At the front of her dorm, she leans toward me and gives me a hug. I'm not expecting it, but it's a welcome, friendly hug.

"So, I'll see you Thursday?" Taylor asks.

"Yeah. Good luck in your scrimmage."

"Thanks."

I stand outside her dorm and watch her as she opens the door and goes inside. Just the way she moves gives me an energy I have never really felt before. It isn't like getting fired up for a football game. I feel completely energized. Maybe my life at Bertram is about to change.

CHAPTER 13

August 26

Today at football practice, for the first time in my life, I have a hard time focusing on football. It's like I'm in a trance. My mind keeps drifting from practice to last night's dinner with Taylor. I keep seeing her face, her body, and those legs. I'm literally thrown back into reality during our defensive practice when I get absolutely laid out by the offensive tackle on the scout team. I see the guard double on our nose guard with the center, but I don't react in time. If you don't fill the hole on the trap, the tackle comes down on you like a thundering mountain. Most offensive tackles weigh about 250 or 260 pounds in high school. Steve Simms is 270 pounds of flesh and only a sophomore. Needless to say, his hit rockets me off my feet and sends me flying, much to the enjoyment of the scout offense. Everyone starts cheering for Steve.

Coach Kaplan comes over and helps me to my feet. "You all right, Morris?"

I adjust my helmet so I'm not looking out my ear hole. "Yeah, I'm okay. I just didn't read the trap block."

"That's not like you. What's on your mind?" he asks knowingly.

"Nothing. I just didn't react in time," I say, re-snapping my chinstrap.

Coach Kaplan shakes his head and says, "Don't let it happen again."

"Don't worry. I won't."

Slapping me on the back of the helmet, he says, "Good idea. Simms 'bout broke you in half."

And with that, my thoughts about Taylor are put on hold. For my own safety, I need to concentrate on what's going on in practice. I finish practice with a few solid tackles and an interception. Coach Kaplan, with his clipboard tucked inside his folded arms, gives me an approving nod. I hope I'm back in his good graces. After practice, I get back to my dorm around three o'clock. As soon as my head hits the pillow, I crash for two hours. Double sessions are bearable, but they definitely take their toll. I'm glad that I'm able to get in a solid power nap before dinner. When I wake up, I see Kevin reading a book in his bed.

"Hey, you want to get some dinner?" he asks.

"Yeah, that sounds great. I'm starving."

Wednesday and Thursday fly by. They are filled with practices, sprints, and more sprints, but I feel like I can run forever. I'm looking forward to our first scrimmage on Friday night. All the while, I'm anticipating my second meeting with Taylor, and at the same time, I can't help thinking about Cindy, and Jack, and Unionville's first game of the season. After Wednesday's practice, I stop by the field hockey field to watch Taylor's scrimmage. I find a discreet spot from which to watch. Taylor steals the ball and flies through the entire defense. She's awesome, fast, and aggressive. I watch for about forty-five minutes, impressed.

Thursday after practice, I meet Taylor at the field hockey field.

She jogs off the field and says, "Hey!"

"How's it going?" I ask.

"The last couple of days have been so busy, but our scrimmage was great. I can't wait until our first game. What about you?"

"Only two more days of doubles, and then we have our first varsity scrimmage." I let out a deep breath. "But I can't stop thinking about Unionville's first game. I miss my friends."

Taylor nods her head. "I know where you're coming from. I left great friends back home, too. It's tough, but it'll get easier once school starts."

"I sure hope so. I met some good guys on the football team, but because I'm playing varsity, I'm stuck between two groups of friends. I play with the seniors, but we're not friends. And the sophomores, I know them better, but I don't play with them. It's like I'm not a part of either group. I feel like the guys only like me because I can play."

Taylor says, "You don't give yourself enough credit. Just give it a chance."

She always seems to say the right thing. I love talking to her, because she makes me feel better. "Hey, thanks for meeting me. I like hanging out with you."

"Yeah," Taylor smiles, "hanging out with you is all right."

Back at her dorm, she gives me another big hug. "Good luck in your scrimmage tomorrow. Only three more days until school starts."

I roll my eyes. "Thanks for reminding me."

Taylor shrugs her shoulders. "It was inevitable."

"Have a good night," I say.

"Yeah, you do the same."

As Taylor walks away, I can feel this force pulling me toward her.

Halfway back to my dorm, I remember that I need to call Cindy. I hurry my pace and get back to my room. I grab my cell phone, walk out onto the campus, and call Cindy. The phone rings and rings until she finally picks up and says, "Hello."

"Hey."

"Oh, hi," Cindy replies half-heartedly.

"What's the matter?"

"Why don't you return my calls?" she answers shortly.

"Cindy," I begin, "I'm sorry. Please don't be mad. I've been busy."

"Busy? You don't have a minute to call?"

"I'm sorry."

She sighs and backs off. "I guess I understand. Things have been busy here, too, but I miss you. It only takes a minute to say hello."

"I know. You're right. I'll do better. Is everything okay?" I ask, trying to change the subject.

"Yeah, but it's hard to believe that school starts next week. My mom and I went shopping today and got some new clothes and school stuff."

"I know, school's right around the corner. How's your mom?"

"She's good. How about your mom?"

It isn't until then that I really think about it, but I haven't talked to my mom since she and Dick dropped me off. "I guess she's okay," I answer. "She's left me some voicemail messages, but I haven't bothered to call her back. She and Dick are probably busy selling the house and moving."

"I'm so sorry," Cindy says. "Are you doing okay? How's your roommate?"

"He's a good guy. We get along okay."

"I'm glad you like him. I was worried you were going to get stuck with some weirdo."

We talk for a while and catch up on all the Unionville gossip. It feels good to talk to her. But even though talking to Cindy makes me feel better, I still can't get Taylor out of my mind. After I hang up, I call Jack to wish him good luck.

I call Jack's number, and he answers, sounding stuffed up. "Hello."

"You okay?" I ask.

"I don't know, man. Things have been tough around here."

"Any news about your mom?"

"She still hasn't come home."

"How are things with your dad?" I ask.

"Listen, man. I don't want to cut you short, but I gotta go."

"What's the matter?"

"Nothing, really, I'm fine."

"I just called to wish you good luck in tomorrow night's game."

"Thanks, man. I gotta go."

"All right," I say. As I hang up the phone, I know something is not right with my best friend. And the worst part is that I'm not there to help him.

CHAPTER 14

August 29–30

It's Friday and almost my last day of summer. It's crazy to think about how much I've been through in the last month. Despite all that's happened, I feel strong, like I can take on the world. I hang out most of the day, feeling anxious about my first varsity scrimmage. I always get super nervous before games.

We are expected to do summer reading, and the book that is assigned for the sophomore class is *The Things They Carried* by Tim O'Brien. I check the book out from the library, but I have a hard time getting started reading it. I'm a slow reader, and I'm distracted by thoughts about our scrimmage. After making it through only the first five pages, I set the book down on my nightstand. Soon after, Kevin walks in.

"What's up, man?" he asks.

"Not much, trying to get some reading done. I hate reading."

"You'll like this book. It's a Vietnam story with lots of violence. You should give it a shot. Besides, it's due Monday."

"I know. I know," I answer. "But I can't stop thinking about tonight, and I can't stop wondering how Unionville is going to do. They play a tough schedule this year. They've got Cincinnati Moeller tonight."

"Yeah, Moeller is tough, but your boys will do fine."

Talking about Unionville's season makes me wish I were playing with them, especially Jack. Taking out my cell phone, I text Jack and Cindy, wishing them good luck as they play and cheer in their first varsity football game.

For the rest of the afternoon, Kevin and I hang out, and I try to read some of my book. Finally, I give up and go for a walk around the campus. The rolling hills are peaceful; the grass is a bright, vibrant green. The trees seem to know that autumn is just around the corner. The smell of football is in the air. As I walk the perimeter of the campus, for the first time since I arrived at Bertram, I notice that it really is an awesome place. The only sounds are the birds chirping, maybe because all the students haven't arrived yet. The football field is lined with bright white paint that almost glows. The stadium is quiet, anticipating greatness. On the football field, I feel like I'm home.

When I get back to the dorm, I grab my stuff, and Kevin and I head to the field house so we can load the bus for our scrimmage. Seniors sit in the back, with Terrance Strong. The juniors come next, and the front of the bus is filled with sophomores. Kevin and I sit together. My headphones pump out my *take no prisoners playlist*. By the time we arrive at the public school down the road, I'm ready to light someone up.

After we warm up, we start the scrimmage on defense. Hudson High School has an offensive line that averages 260 pounds. The players are big, strong, and, as I quickly discover, fast. When the ball is first snapped, it seems like everything is kicked into fast-forward. Practice was one thing, but during the scrimmage, everything seems like a blur. The jump from freshman football to varsity football is insane and super fast. Because it's a scrimmage, Hudson's offense runs ten plays in a row. I feel lost, like I have never played the game before. I start to question myself. Maybe I'm not cut out for varsity football.

Terrance comes up behind me and hits my shoulder pads. I turn around, and he grabs my facemask. Looking into my eyes, into my soul, he says, "Hey, Morris. What the hell are you doin'? You haven't made a play yet. Why don't you show us what you Unionville boys are all about? You got more game than that."

Unionville boys. The thought of all my friends back home gets me fired up. I promised not to let them down, especially Jack. During the first series, I manage to hold my own. By the second set of ten plays, I have adjusted to the speed of the game. On the first three plays, I make two solo tackles and have an assist. After stepping in front of a tight-end dump pass and making an interception, I'm mobbed by my new teammates, led by Terrance Strong.

After the scrimmage, Coach Carlson comes up to me and says, "You did a nice job out there today. I'm real proud of you. Keep up the good work, and stay humble. Big egos are the death of good athletes."

Kevin and I talk about the scrimmage on the way home. He got in and played some nose guard, and I got to run the ball with the second-string offense and scored a touchdown. When the bus pulls onto the long driveway at Bertram, I'm glad to be back and to have my first varsity experience under my belt, but I can't wait to find out how Unionville did in its first official game. When I get back, I grab my cell phone to call Jack and Cindy. It's only ten o'clock, but neither one of them answers. Frustrated, I try sending a few texts, but I can't reach either one of them. I get into bed, anxious to see tomorrow's paper in the library. I'll be the first one there to grab the sports page.

My alarm goes off at 7:00 a.m. Throwing on some sweatpants and my baseball hat, I walk to the library where I find Saturday's paper on the shelf. I search through it, looking for the sports page, but it's nowhere to be found. Discouraged, I look around the library, only to find Taylor sitting in a chair in the corner of the room, glancing over the top of Saturday's sports page.

"Are you looking for this?" she mocks. She's wearing her field hockey warm-ups and a baseball hat, looking super cute.

"Yes, yes, I am," I answer, willing to play along.

"How much is it worth to you?" she teases.

"Anything you want," I promise.

She smiles and continues, "Looks like your Unionville boys are a team to be reckoned with. They pounded the number-two ranked team in the state, and they're only Division II."

My eyes widen. "Really? Can I see that?"

Taylor hands me the paper, and, sure enough, Unionville did win, 28–7.

THE DAYTON FLYER
High School Football: WEEK 1

The Unionville Rockets started their season with an impressive 28–7 win over #2 state-ranked Cincinnati Moeller. The offense was led by sophomore tailback Jack Thompson. Thompson, who was moved from the fullback position, ran like a man possessed. He carried the ball 24 times for 220 yards and three touchdowns. By the end of the night, Moeller didn't even want to try to tackle him. The final score was a pass from senior quarterback Danny Towers to Woody Fletcher. Towers finished the night 18 for 24 for 260 yards. The Rockets totaled over 500 yards in total offense. The defense shut down Moeller, who only scored one touchdown late in the fourth quarter. Unionville looks forward to their next game against cross-town rival, Iron City.

Jack never mentioned that Coach Murphy moved him from fullback to tailback. He probably didn't want me to feel bad. I can't believe I'm missing all of this.

"Are you okay?" Taylor asks. "Aren't you happy for them?"

"Yeah, I'm fine, but I wish I were part of that team." I point to the article in the paper. "I'm supposed to be there."

"There's nothing you can do about it. You're here, and they're there. Don't have any regrets." She shakes her head. "You'll be sorry if you do."

I look at Taylor and think about what she said. I don't know how to feel, but I know that what she said makes sense. The reality is that I'm at Bertram, whether I like it or not. I try to convince myself that if I work hard and do the best that I can, everything will be fine. "You know what?" I say to Taylor, folding the newspaper in half. "You're right."

Taylor takes the paper out of my hand. "What do you say we get some breakfast and celebrate that awesome interception you had in your scrimmage?"

I do a double take and look at Taylor. "How did you know about my interception?"

"Mary Jo, one of my girlfriends on the field hockey team, has a car. Her boyfriend is Mike Giffin. You probably know him. He's your starting quarterback. Mary Jo was going to go to the scrimmage because it was so close by, and I asked her if I could go."

I must be smiling from ear to ear, because Taylor just laughs.

"Thanks for coming. I appreciate it."

"Well, maybe there's another reason you ended up at Bertram, other than football." She grabs my hat off my head and runs. I chase after her, and I'm surprised to find that I have a hard time catching up. We race to the cafeteria for some breakfast and to talk about the scrimmage and my first varsity football game, which is less than a week away.

Taylor says, "School's only two days away. Did you do your summer reading?"

"I don't like to read," I say, chomping down on some pancakes.

"You might want to think about starting off on the right foot."

"Thanks for the advice, but I think I'll be okay."

We sit for about twenty minutes, hanging out and talking until Taylor says, "I have some things I need to get done. I have a scrimmage tomorrow evening, but I'll see you in school on Monday."

"Okay, I'll see you later." I stop her and say, "Thanks for the good advice."

Taylor gets up from the table and says, "Don't go soft on me, Billy Morris. You've got some football to play and a book to read."

I take another bite of my pancakes, and with a full mouth I say, "Book? What book?"

CHAPTER 15

September 1

English is my first class of the day. Walking down the hallway, I'm relieved to see familiar faces from the football team. It definitely makes things easier. I'm even more excited when I see Taylor walking toward the same classroom. She catches my eye and says, "Hey, how's it going?"

"Okay, I guess."

"Did you finish reading?" Taylor asks.

"I got through the first couple of chapters," I admit.

"Seriously?" I can hear the disappointment in her voice.

Shrugging my shoulders, I say, "In Unionville, I never had to read. I just didn't do it."

Taylor rolls her eyes. "Come on. We'd better get to class."

We choose seats next to each other in the back of the room. As soon as we sit down, the teacher comes in. The loud talking among the students dwindles to one or two random conversations.

The teacher waits until everyone is quiet and introduces himself. "My name is Mr. Tanner, and I'll be your English teacher this year. This is tenth-grade English, just in case anyone is not sure he or she is in the right place."

After he introduces himself, he moves around the room like a drill sergeant inspecting his troops. His steel-blue eyes are intimidating and seem to look right through us. He has everyone introduce themselves to the rest of the class. When it comes to me, I say my name and where I'm from. All eyes are on the new kid. I feel like I'm all alone on an island, until I look over at Taylor and remember she's in the same boat. I'm glad that Taylor is here.

Mr. Tanner assigns seats. I'm disappointed that Taylor is now on the other side of the room. Mr. Tanner begins his lecture. His excitement is evident when he starts class with a discussion about *The Things They Carried*. "Tim O'Brien's writing is as authentic as it comes, from first-hand experiences. Because I fought in Vietnam, this unit is important to me on a personal level." Tanner paces around the room, pointing out passages from the book and bringing the intensity of the battlefield right into our class.

Mr. Tanner asks, "Can anyone shed some light on this summer's reading assignment? What did the book tell you about how soldiers felt about being in Vietnam? How did those feelings change after their first couple of weeks in-country? Let me see here." He scans his seating chart. "Mr. Morris?"

My paperback is neatly placed on the upper right hand corner of the desk, without any sign of use. I look up, not believing the chances of him calling on me, and I tentatively respond, "I, uh, did not do the reading."

There is a chuckle from some of the students around me. Clearly, I'm the dumb jock. Trying to redirect the class's attention, I say, "I think the girl in the back of the room knows the answer." One girl waves her hand violently in the back row.

After giving me a penetrating stare, Mr. Tanner shifts his attention to the other side of the room and calls on another student. During the rest of the class, I slouch down in my chair. Like a turtle sliding back into his shell, I try to remain out of sight. My first day of school is off to a miserable start. My blood boils when I think about my mom and how she got me into this mess.

Mr. Tanner's class seems to last an eternity, and when class winds down, he looks directly at me and says, "There will be a written test over the material during tomorrow's class."

So I have football practice and an entire novel to read … tonight.

Mr. Tanner dismisses the class. As the students filter out of the room, he pulls me aside and says, "Mr. Morris, I want a word with you." When the last student leaves the classroom, Tanner closes the door and moves into my personal space. Towering over me, he looks down and says in a low and serious tone, "Mr. Morris, I don't know why your reading isn't done, but know this—I can be your best ally or your worst enemy. See to it that you do the work in my class." He moves his face only inches from mine, and as he moves back into drill sergeant mode, his voice thunders when he says, "I do not want to have this conversation again. *Is that clear?*"

I look at Mr. Tanner wide-eyed, not knowing what to say. I've never had a teacher talk to me like that. I manage to respond, "Yes, sir. I'll do the work."

As the day wears on, I discover that Bertram is more of a challenge than I ever could have imagined. My second period is French class. At Unionville, I took French for three years, and I thought I knew the language pretty well. But at Bertram, the second year French teacher doesn't say one word in English. I'm in way over my head in that class. From there, I head to Art class, not one of my stronger subjects. Our Art teacher, Mr. McDaniel, explains that we have to draw a landscape of the campus. We sit outside with our drawing pencils and these giant boards. At one point, Mr. McDaniel looks over my shoulder. He pulls his long black hair into a ponytail and asks me, "What is it that you got there?"

I try to explain, "Um, that's that tree over there, and that's that building."

"I see," he says. At least he seems patient, friendly, like a hippie from the 1960s.

My schedule reads that my fourth period is a *free period*. I don't even know what that is. At Unionville, we had study halls. I start walking around the campus to ask someone what a free period is. There's a student center, where some students hang out. It's at this point that I feel completely out of place. I don't see anyone from the football team. Students are all over the campus doing homework, playing Frisbee, reading books. Finally, I get the nerve to ask a student who is sitting on the lawn doing some math homework. "Excuse me," I say.

A boy with medium length brown hair looks up from his math book.

"What's a free period?" I ask.

He explains, "During your free period, your time is your time, to do what you want. Some kids hang out. I try to get as much of my homework done so I don't have to do it at after school."

"Thanks, man," I say. The first thing that pops into my mind is reading *The Things They Carried*. Then, I feel a tap on my shoulder. It's Taylor. Man, am I glad to see her.

"Hey, are you making it through the day?" she asks.

"I guess, but it's harder than I thought it would be. These classes are impossible."

"Yeah, I've been pretty busy, too, but I'm excited," Taylor explains.

"What are you so excited about?"

A big smile stretches across Taylor's face. "I just had my music class. My teacher's amazing. I think that she can teach me a lot about the violin. It's kinda why I'm here."

"That's cool. But I just have one question—what's the deal with free periods?" I laugh.

"Yeah, awesome, huh? Maybe you should get some reading done."

We find a spot under a big maple tree in front of the large building that serves as the campus cafeteria.

While I read my book, Taylor does some of her Spanish homework. Surprising even myself, I manage to read a few chapters of the novel before Taylor and I go to lunch together. Despite the fact that I hate reading, I find myself getting interested in the story.

My afternoon is filled with three classes. In Geometry, I have to learn the first five theorems and do twenty sample problems for homework. My science class is Biology, where we study the anatomy of the frog. I have to read chapters one through three. Tomorrow we get to begin dissecting our own frog. Lucky us. The last class of the day is World History. Our homework is to read the first two chapters in our textbook. The teachers seem nice, but Bertram is very different from Unionville. The teachers are more like professors, and the students never goof off. The students are focused, dedicated. On my way over to the gym to get ready for practice, I see Taylor and catch up to her.

"I see you survived," she jokes.

"Barely," I respond. "I didn't know this was the Ivy League."

She nods her head. "You'll adjust."

"I hope so. Maybe I'll talk to you later?"

Taylor stops me and says, "I can help you study for the summer reading test if you want."

"I'm in. How about the library at eight?"

Taylor says, "I'll see you then."

Monday's practice is light. We do some jogging and watch some film of our first opponents, the Twinsburg Tigers, the Division I state runner-up from last year. Even though I try to focus on practice, my mind is filled with thoughts of my first day of school and my encounter with Mr. Tanner.

I have only read through the first eight chapters of the book, leaving me with seventeen more to go. Our practice ends early, so I go to my dorm and try to get as much reading done as I can. After grabbing some food at the cafeteria, I make my way to the library to meet Taylor.

Taylor is in the back of the library in her usual casual warm-up attire with her cherry-red Ohio State baseball hat.

"Hey, Billy," she flirts. "Are you ready to get to work?"

"Yeah," I reply, "I got some of the reading done after practice. I only have about ninety pages to go."

We find a study table, and we talk a little bit about the book. With Taylor's help and after being threatened by Mr. Tanner, I've never been more focused. Apparently, intimidation is a very effective teaching tool. Taylor's explanation makes things easier to understand. We read the last five chapters out loud to each other. It takes us almost an hour, but I feel ready for tomorrow's test.

"You have a great reading voice," Taylor comments. "You should join the debate team or something."

I laugh. "Maybe I should just worry about passing this test tomorrow."

Taylor nods her head. "Yeah, you're right, baby steps."

"What do you have the rest of the week?" I ask Taylor.

"Well, let's see. I have a violin recital on Thursday. And, oh yeah, I'm going to try to make it to your game on Friday. Mary Jo said that she is going to drive."

"That's cool. I'll go to your recital on Thursday."

A small smile appears on Taylor's face. "It's a deal."

"Hey, thanks for helping me with all of this school stuff. You know you don't have to."

"I know I don't have to, but maybe we'll both do better by helping each other."

Tuesday morning, Mr. Tanner hands me the test. I take it and answer each question, knowing that my responses are correct. It is the beginning of my new approach to school. My week is a mixture of classes, practices, Taylor's game, and her violin recital.

On Thursday night, I go to Taylor's recital. Settling in the back of the auditorium, I look over the program. Next to Taylor's name it reads: *Bach's Lullaby*. I never had an appreciation for classical music or the violin until I see Taylor alone on that stage, under the spotlight. Each note is distinct, perfect. Her brown hair glistens and blends perfectly with the wood of the violin. In the back of the auditorium, I'm swept away by the music, riding on each note, wondering how I could be so lucky to have met a girl like Taylor.

Friday morning rolls around, the day of my first varsity football game under the lights. I try to focus in my classes, but I can't. All I can think about is what's to come. I'm nervous as hell.

CHAPTER 16

September 5

A ball of rage sits in the pit of my stomach, and I'm ready to explode. Standing in front of the mirror in Twinsburg's visiting team's locker room, I apply eyeblack under my eyes, completing my gladiator's uniform. My helmet is red with a gray eagle on either side. We are wearing our white jerseys with red numbers and our gray pants. Wearing my favorite number, 22, I have completed my transformation into a warrior. Even though the nerves have set in, I feel confident because I know that no one on our team has worked harder for this opportunity. I can't help but think about all those summer workouts with Jack, running those bleachers, and lifting all those weights. This is my time.

I tape my wrists with athletic tape from the trainer, my pregame ritual. Kevin walks up to me and pounds his fists on my shoulder pads. "Are you ready?" he shouts, all fired up.

I just nod my head. I have already put myself into a different state of mind.

Bertram has prepared for bigger games than this one, but to me, it's the biggest game of my life. I have a lot to prove.

Coach Carlson calls the team together, and we huddle in the middle of the locker room. We are a team.

"No fear," Coach Carlson begins. "We have spent the last few weeks preparing for this. Have no fear, because preparation and dedication erase all that. Your teammates erase all that. The person next to you will not let you down, and you will not let him down. Pick each other up. Be relentless. Be courageous. Play together and play hard. Make sure when this game is over, you have left everything on the field. Men, if you do that, I promise you, you will be victorious. This is when all the hard work you have invested since the beginning of January, over the summer, and the last few weeks of double sessions pays off. It's time to withdraw that investment. Believe that your hard work will be rewarded today. Captains, get everyone together. *Get it done. Let's bring home a victory.*"

A chill shoots through my body. The captains lead our team in reciting the Lord's Prayer. Cleats scrape along the floor of the locker room, as we form two lines side by side. Kevin and I are partners. As we exit the locker room, I slide my helmet over my head like Russell Crowe in *Gladiator*, ready for battle.

From the corner of the end zone, we jog to the fifty-yard line and then get into our stretching positions. The Tigers are wearing their white pants and blue jerseys. Their white helmets have blue numbers on one side and a tiger paw on the other. Their linemen are closest to midfield, and they seem larger than life. All I think to myself is *No Fear*. The stands are packed with students and parents. During our warm-up routine, the captains go to midfield for the coin toss. The referee uniforms glow bright white and solid black, brand new for the first game of the season. Terrance returns to the team to tell us that we won the toss and deferred to the second half. We will be starting on defense, but first, we will have to kick off. As a headhunter on the kickoff team, my job is to bust the blocking wedge.

Slapping my hands on my thigh pads, I dig my cleats into the ground. The kickoff turns end over end and is caught by their return man, who is also their starting tailback, Scott Salyers. The scouting reports say he isn't big, only five feet six inches, but he is an All-State track athlete. Running full speed toward the mass of bodies, I hurl myself at the first man leading the wedge. The popping of the pads echoes throughout the stadium, and I destroy the first man. The contact is solid. The adrenaline pumps through my body. The blocking wedge disintegrates. Kevin flies in from the side, putting a solid hit on Scott and taking him down. The first defense sprints out onto the field. During the kickoff, my left forearm gets gashed on a helmet. But it doesn't faze me. Pulling my wristband over the cut, I ignore it, loving the contact, the battle, and the high.

Taking my place as the inside linebacker in our base 52 defense, I make calls to my defensive linemen: "Stick 52, Ram, Ram," calling a slant to the right. Their quarterback, an All-State basketball player, comes to the line of scrimmage and looks over the defense. I peer into his eyes from behind my facemask. He seems calm, relaxed. The fire in my gut burns hotter.

He shouts out the signals: "Blue 20... Blue 20... Set... Hut!" The ball is snapped. I read the guard doubling on the nose; the play is a fullback trap. Shooting into the gap, I meet the fullback head-on. The contact is solid as my shoulder rams into his thigh. Wrapping my arms around his legs and lifting, I drive him into the hard-packed earth. He groans on impact. Another shot of adrenaline shoots through my body. I no longer feel human. Mobbed by my team, I'm slapped on the helmet in celebration of the big hit.

Coach Kaplan signals in defenses to Marcus Tyler and shouts encouragement. He is completely engaged on the sideline with his headphones and clipboard, barking in the referee's ear, "Watch the holding! Their left tackle is holding our defensive end! Throw the flag! Do your job!"

On the next play, the quarterback drops back and breaks contain. He begins to scramble and heads for our sidelines. Taking a perfect angle, I run him down for a two-yard loss. Marcus slaps me on the helmet and shouts, "Way to go, baby!"

On third down and twelve, Twinsburg's quarterback drops back and throws a ball that sails over the head of his wide receiver. Twinsburg lines up to punt on fourth down. Terrance is the deep man, and I stand ten yards in front of him as his lead blocker.

"You ready, Morris?" he yells. "Let's make it happen!"

"Let's do it!" I shout back.

Terrance receives the punt and follows my lead. After I throw a punishing block on the first man, he makes two people miss and almost breaks it for a touchdown. Twinsburg will have its hands full containing Terrance Strong.

Even though Twinsburg has a solid returning team, Terrance runs through and jumps over their defense. On the few occasions that his wiry and elusive frame does not make the corner on a sweep, he lowers his shoulder and punishes the defender, surprising him with his strength. On one play, he starts running to the right, cuts all the way back across the field, and ends up on the left side of the field, in the end zone, for a touchdown. I'm glad Terrance is on our team. By the end of the night, the Twinsburg players are fighting with each other, pointing fingers. Terrance finishes the night with 189 yards rushing on only eighteen carries. He scores three touchdowns. Our defense doesn't give up a single point. Twinsburg only manages to cross the fifty-yard line one time.

We win, 21–0.

Coach Carlson brings us together in the locker room, a scene not that different from the beginning of the game. He says, "Even though we are a smaller-division school, we took it to 'em. We played together as a team. Every aspect of our game was solid. We were better prepared, in better shape, hungrier. Men, this is just the beginning. Game one is over. Enjoy it. We'll get back to work on Monday for game two. Remember, one game at a time."

In my first varsity game as a starting sophomore, I have eight tackles, one sack, and an interception. I take it all in: playing under the lights, the roar of the crowd, the feeling of being invincible. But even those feelings and the winning and the stats aren't satisfying. Even though I love the game of football and the feeling I get inside, the adrenaline, the natural high, I can feel in my heart that something is missing. My first varsity win is an empty one. Sitting on the bus, in the middle of all that excitement, I think about my friends back in Unionville.

Instead of celebrating a victory with Bertram, I think about Woody Fletcher and the good times we used to have riding our bikes around town. How Woody and I have been friends since first grade. I think about Jack and how we used to stay up all night making wings and playing hours and hours of PlayStation. This victory with Bertram isn't even close to what it felt like to win at Unionville with my best friends.

As the school bus rolls out of the parking lot, I can't help but wish that I were playing for Unionville. More than anything, I miss being with my friends.

CHAPTER 17
September 6

I jump out of bed and race to the library to get Saturday's paper, only to find Taylor waiting for me. On the way over, I had hoped she would be here.

Taylor says, "I figured you'd show up here, wanting to know how Unionville did last night. By the way, great game! You were awesome!"

I can't help but smile at Taylor. "Thanks for coming."

"You did a good job," she says, while handing me the sports page. It's already turned to the article about Unionville's second game.

THE DAYTON FLYER
High School Football: WEEK 2

The Unionville Rockets increased their record to 2–0 by overpowering Iron City, 42–7. Once again, Unionville was led by the hard running and tackling of sophomore tailback and linebacker Jack Thompson.

Thompson scored four rushing touchdowns for the Rockets. He ran for 195 yards on 30 carries. He was the workhorse for the Rockets. On defense, he dominated with 14 tackles. Danny Towers continued to demonstrate his strength at the quarterback position by throwing for 280 yards and two touchdowns. Iron City never got in the game. The Rockets came out pounding the ball. Led by a strong and fast offensive line, Thompson punished would-be-tacklers and scored three of his four touchdowns in the first half. Unionville will face Dayton Dunbar next Friday night.

I look at Taylor and say, "Man, Jack is playing great. I gotta call him."

Taylor nods her head. "You must be excited for him."

"I just wish I was with him—in the backfield. We should be playing together."

Taylor points at me. "You should call him."

"I'm going to try right now. You want to meet later for lunch?"

"I'll meet you at noon in front of the cafeteria."

Taking my phone out of my pocket, I head out onto the campus and call Jack, listening to the ringing as I walk toward the football field.

Jack answers. "Billy!"

"Hey, man."

"It seems like I haven't talked to you for the longest time. How are things going?" Jack asks.

It is good to hear Jack's voice. "I'm doing okay. Last night was amazing, but my first varsity football game wasn't how I pictured it. I always thought it would be with you guys, wearing the blue and gold."

"I know what you mean. It's not the same without you."

Jack's words cut into me. It hits me how much I really miss being there, how much I miss my friends, especially my best friend.

"I've been reading the sports page. Seven touchdowns already! Sounds like all that work is paying off."

"Yeah, man. It's an awesome feeling, running into the end zone, looking up at all the fans. I was nervous before the game started, but once I scored that first touchdown, it was like I was in control. I felt like no one could tackle me, like I was unstoppable. Everyone on the team is coming together."

A lump sits in my throat. "How is everything else?"

I hear Jack take a deep breath on the other end of the line.

"You doin' okay?" I ask again.

His excited tone turns quiet. "Things at home are tough. My mom still hasn't come back, and my old man got a DUI last Friday after the football game and spent the weekend in jail. He's meeting with his lawyer today. He's been drinking every night. Last Thursday, before our first game, he came home from the bar drunk, pulled me out of bed, and started pushing me around. He bruised one of my ribs. I could barely breathe. I wasn't going to play last week."

"But you had an awesome game. How did you do it?"

"I took everything out on Moeller. Punished 'em. Those dudes wanted nothing to do with me. I figure for every punch my dad dished out, I would make those guys pay. It was like I was possessed or something. Even Coach Murphy asked me if I was all right."

"What did you tell him?"

"I told him I was all fired up, first varsity game and all that. He ate it up."

"What can I do?" I ask.

"It'll work itself out."

"Are you sure?"

"You got enough going on," Jack reminds me.

"You know, I haven't even talked to my mom since she dropped me off, more than three weeks ago," I say, realizing how long it's been.

"I saw her and Dick just the other day. They sold the house. She's moving down to South Carolina next week. She said she's been calling you, leaving messages on your phone. Says you never answer it."

"I know. I don't feel like talking to her."

"Billy, my mom left, and I haven't been able to talk to her. I would do anything to talk to her. At least you can still talk to your mom."

"Yeah, I guess you're right."

Jack quickly changes the subject. "Hey, man. How tough are those guys at Bertram?"

"Some of the guys are really tough. They're from all over. Most of them transferred here after their freshman year. Some are bad dudes, hard hitters, and fast. They play the game like it's supposed to be played. Terrance Strong is the real deal, talks about going pro all the time, already has college recruiters coming to the games. One coach sent him a five-page handwritten letter telling him how much he wanted him at Florida State."

"No kidding," Jack says with excitement in his voice. "That's awesome."

"It's pretty cool. This whole group of seniors is like professionals, you know, the way they prepare for games and things like that. It's easy to see how they won state last year."

Jack says, "Speaking of that, did you know we could play in the playoffs? Unionville and Bertram are both in Division II. Could you imagine playing against each other? I would totally crush you."

"Yeah, right. I would knock you down!" I say.

"Whatever, but just think, it could happen."

"Well, we'll see. The season just started."

"I know, but it's something to think about," Jack says.

"Yeah, you're right." Talking to Jack makes me feel better. "Hey, man. Can we do a better job of keeping in touch? If you ever need to talk to somebody about your dad or anything, call me. Don't go it alone, man. You don't have to. That's what friends are for."

"I know. Things have been nuts. Leigh and I fight all the time. She says that I'm always pissed off. We got in this huge fight after last night's game. I got all drunk at Danny's house. His parents were out of town, so we went there after the game. She saw me all wasted and said I was acting like an idiot. She says I'm changing, that I'm not the guy I used to be. She's been threatening to break up with me. To be honest, I don't care what she does."

"She cares about you."

"The only thing I've got in my life right now is football. It's my outlet. It's the only place I can go to get away from all of this. When I'm on the field, I become someone else. You know, I put that helmet on, and all of a sudden, I'm in control."

"I know how you feel. It's the only time I feel like I belong at Bertram. It's the only time I feel normal." Pausing for a moment, I say, "Until I met this girl."

"Dude, who is she? Is she hot?"

"Taylor. She's got brown hair. She's all tan, perfect smile. Plays the violin, sings, and acts. She's on the field hockey team."

"That's great, man, but what about Cindy? She's been asking about you."

"I don't know what to do. I don't know how to tell her that this long distance relationship isn't going to work."

"You have to tell her how you feel. If you drag it out, it's only going to make things worse."

"I know. You're right, but that doesn't make it any easier. I don't want to hurt her feelings."

"You're just hurting her worse by dragging it out. She'll get over it."

"I don't think she would understand the things I've been through. Taylor is amazing. She always says the right things. When I talk to her, I feel like we've known each other forever. She knows everything about me, and she doesn't think I'm crazy."

Jack laughs. "Not many girls would put up with either one of us."

"You got that right. I'll figure it out. I won't drag things out."

"Listen, man. My dad's going to be back soon, and I don't want to be here when he gets back. I'm going to meet Leigh. Good job last night."

"Yeah, you, too. I'll talk to you soon. Don't be a stranger, like the rest of the guys back in Unionville. You know I haven't talked to a single one of them."

"It's tough finding out who your real friends are."

We say goodbye, and I hang up the phone. Standing way out on the soccer fields, I start thinking about how I've lost contact with so many of my other friends: Woody, Jacob, and Tombo. I think about how quickly my good friends slipped away. I think about watching *The Longest Yard* in Tombo's basement until the sun came up. Then there's Woody Fletcher and the good times we used to have riding our bikes into town and buying burgers with spare change at Mills' Diner. And then there's Jacob Conroy, with whom I played little league baseball, singing songs in his mom's minivan on the way home. When I was in eighth grade, I figured I had twenty best friends. By ninth grade, I had maybe ten good buddies. And here I am, a year later, with only one person I can rely on and call my friend.

CHAPTER 18

September 7–8

I decide to check the messages on my phone that my mother has left since I arrived at Bertram. The messages are short, but I can tell by the tone of her voice that she is concerned about me and irritated that I haven't called her back. She and Dick have found a temporary apartment and are looking for a new house in South Carolina. She says that the weather is beautiful and that she can't wait until I come to visit.

I'm not interested in my mother's invitation. I feel a resentment that I find hard to describe. There she is, living her life, and here I am, living my life and trying to make the best out of my situation at Bertram. Every day, I miss my friends and my old life in Unionville. There was so much I had planned for, had worked for. I try to understand what I did to deserve all this. I resent my mom and Dick.

As I play my mom's last message, Kevin comes into the room and sits down. He looks tired and bummed.

"What's up?" I ask.

"It's nothing, really," Kevin says, plopping his head back on his pillow.

"Dude, you look miserable."

Kevin takes a deep breath. "I thought this was going to be a new beginning for me."

"What are you talking about? You've been doing awesome. You got some varsity time at nose guard, and you're only a sophomore."

"You don't understand. My dad can be a real jerk sometimes. He puts so much pressure on me, I feel like I'm going to burst."

"Why's he doing that?"

"I don't know. He picked up and moved our whole family here from Iron City. He thought this would be my opportunity to get a scholarship somewhere. You know, play college ball. He's a high school teacher and doesn't make much money. He said I would have to pay for college on my own."

Kevin has changed since we arrived. He's not as friendly, and he's less patient. Kevin is a good athlete, but he's flighty on the football field, so the coaches haven't put him in an important position where he has to make a lot of decisions. At nose guard, all he has to do is try to beat the center and get into the backfield. With his speed and strength, he's a great nose guard.

Kevin looks at me with tired eyes. "What am I going to do?"

"It's only your sophomore year. This team is mostly juniors and seniors. There are only three starters who aren't seniors. You'll get your chance."

Kevin sits up and says, "I wish my dad saw it that way. He pisses me off. I wish he could see that I was doing my best and stop putting so much pressure on me. Some of the players are starting to give me a hard time."

"I didn't realize things were so tough." Even though we are roommates, Kevin rarely shares the things that are going on in his life. I reassure him, "Things will get better."

But things for Kevin don't get better. In fact, they get a whole lot worse. After practice on Monday, the seniors get him. They start their ritual of taping unsuspecting sophomores, and because Kevin's dad has been running his mouth in the stands about how Kevin should be starting, they pick Kevin to be their first victim. They use about ten rolls of white athletic tape swiped from the trainer and wrap him up like a mummy.

The hazing ritual is underway before I get back to the locker room, which is about a half mile from the field. When I walk into the locker room, I see six seniors carrying a mummy into the gym. Kevin yells, *"Put me down!"* He grunts every bad word there is and fights back, kicking and shouting, but without any luck. The other sophomores skip showers and get out of the locker room, ignoring his yells for help, saving themselves.

I run toward Kevin, where I am met by half the offensive line. One of the offensive linemen puts out his hand and says, "This ain't your problem, Morris. Just go about your business."

I try to get to Kevin. I try to help him, but the linemen stand in the way. Because I'm outmatched, I reluctantly go back to my locker. Eventually, they take Kevin to the gymnasium, and I follow them.

A few of the seniors slide him into the gym. Because his feet are still bound together, Kevin struggles to get up and hop out of the gym. Tears run down his face, and fury burns in his eyes.

I run over to Kevin and start removing the tape. He pushes me away. "Get off me!" he grunts. "Don't touch me!"

"I was out at the field. I tried to help."

"Leave me the hell alone," he mutters, while pulling the tape from the hair on his head and legs. The tape pulls hard on the hair, and he's shaking.

If his father only knew that he brought all of this onto his son—if he only knew. This wasn't even Kevin's fault. He's a good guy who works hard, keeps his mouth shut, and tries to do his best. His father pushes him too hard and runs his mouth in the stands to the other parents. I can't even begin to understand the anger and embarrassment that Kevin must feel. He grabs his equipment and walks out the back door of the locker room.

The next day at practice, the team sees a very different side of Coach Carlson. His eyes narrow when he says, "You guys think you're tough. What was it, ten seniors on one sophomore? Shameful, embarrassing, ridiculous. Is that the way to treat another member of the team? Is that the way to be a team?"

Coach Carlson knows the seniors are responsible, but he probably isn't sure exactly who participated. He can't suspend the entire senior class plus a handful of juniors. *"We are a team! We are a team!"* The words echo throughout the locker room. "Those of you who participated in yesterday's hazing should be ashamed. This stops *now*. If I so much as hear of anything resembling hazing, you will be removed not just from the team but from Bertram. *Is that clear?"* Coach Carlson's face has turned a dark shade of red.

Everyone responds, "Yes, Coach." The room is silent except for the dripping water coming from the showers. Coach's words have sunk in. Many of the seniors have their heads down, realizing they went beyond what they thought was a practical joke.

After practice, Coach Carlson keeps all the seniors. They start on the goal line with bear crawls. Every ten yards, they get to their feet and do ten grass drills. Two hundred yards and 200 grass drills later, I'm sure the seniors have started to understand what they did was wrong.

After practice, I walk back to the locker room with Kevin. He seems to be doing better. I tell him, "Listen, man. I'm sorry about yesterday."

"I don't want to hear it. It's not going to be okay. No thanks to you."

"Come on, Kevin. There was nothing I could do."

Kevin shakes his head. "I have to live with this, not you!"

I can see in Kevin's eyes that he wants revenge, and he wants nothing to do with me.

I decide to leave Kevin alone. Being roommates with Kevin is not going to be easy. And me, well, I just went from having two friends at Bertram to now only having one.

On the way back to the dorm, I run into Taylor, who has just finished field hockey practice. She jogs over to me with her usual smile. I don't smile back.

"What's the matter?" she asks.

I tell her the whole story about Kevin.

She shakes her head. "He must be humiliated. He seems like such a good guy."

"Yeah, he really is. I think he just needs some time to get over it."

"Just be his friend. Don't get frustrated if he won't talk to you."

"I think I can do that," I say, relieved to be able to talk to Taylor.

"Hey," she says, "don't forget, we have a test tomorrow in English."

"Yeah, I know. I've been studying. I promised Tanner."

I return to my dorm, feeling bad for Kevin and thinking about Taylor. I know that I feel something for her, something I have never felt before. She makes me feel good about myself; she makes me feel alive.

The realization sets in that I have to figure out a way to break up with Cindy, even though I know she'll be hurt.

At about 7:30 p.m., I walk toward the baseball fields and call Cindy. The September sun is still warm.

"Hey," a quiet voice answers.

"Hey, Cindy."

"I've been thinking about you. I was hoping you'd call."

This is going to be harder than I thought. It wasn't that long ago that I was convinced that I was falling for Cindy.

After a long silence, Cindy says, "Hello? Are you there?"

"Yeah, yeah, I'm here. I'm out at the baseball fields. How have you been? How's cheerleading?"

"It's good," Cindy says. "School has been busy with practice and games and all that. The first few weeks of school have flown by. I'm always thinking about you, wondering how you're doing."

"I'm doing okay. Football's been good. My English teacher is really intense, and my other classes are impossible. My head's been spinning from the schoolwork."

"Sounds like Bertram is tough. School here is good. I actually have some pretty cool teachers this year. Cheerleading's been awesome."

"That's really good."

"You know, I was thinking that maybe I could come up to see your first home game this weekend. What do you think?" Cindy asks.

"Cindy?" My brain spins.

"Yeah, what's up?"

"I don't think that's such a good idea."

"How come?" she asks, sounding disappointed.

Taking a deep breath, I look out over the vacant baseball field from my seat, now high on the top row of the bleachers. "You're a great friend. I want to stay friends, but I need to figure some things out."

"Billy, did I do something wrong?"

My heart pounds, and my stomach aches. "I feel like I have too much going on right now, and I feel bad when I don't have a chance to call you. I think we should go our separate ways."

"I don't want to lose you. We can make this work," Cindy says, now sounding more angry than sad.

"We can still be friends."

"Friends? Really? You've got to be kidding!"

"It doesn't have to end this way."

"You want to know something? I thought you were better than this."

"Cindy?"

"I gotta go." She hangs up the phone.

Sitting on the bleachers, it isn't sadness that I feel, but rather a sense of relief, like a giant burden has been lifted off my shoulders. I won't have to feel guilty about talking to Taylor, and I won't feel bad about not calling Cindy. I tell myself that Cindy will be fine, that it will just take some time.

I sit looking down at my phone and then I call Jack, hoping I can get a hold of him, because I need a good friend to talk to.

"Billy," Jack answers.

"What's up, man?"

"Not much. You?"

"I just broke up with Cindy," I say.

"You did what? Unbelievable."

"I know. I feel bad. I'm sure she hates me."

"Ah, man, don't worry about it. She'll be fine."

"I didn't want to hurt her."

"She's cool; she'll get over it." Jack tries to reassure me. "Listen, man. You did the right thing. You were just being honest with her."

"Yeah, I guess you're right." Trying to change the subject, I say, "So, how are you and things in Unionville?"

"My old man is out at the bar. He already has that DUI, so now he walks up to The Tavern. He's officially the town drunk."

I try to understand his life. I feel bad because I'm not there to help him. "I wish I could do something."

"Yeah, me, too. Leigh and I got in another huge fight about my drinking. She told me I'm just like my old man."

"What did you say to her?"

"I told her that she didn't have a clue what my dad was like and that she should mind her own business. I haven't talked to her since. She won't even look at me at school."

"What are you going to do?"

"Don't know."

"Are you okay?"

"It just gets frustrating, everybody talking about my dad. It seems like everyone is making my life their business. Even Coach Murphy was asking about how I was doing at home."

"How do you deal with all that?"

"I live with it every day. Last night the bartender at The Tavern called here and told me to come get my dad, because he could barely stand up, on a Monday night."

"Keep doing the best you can at school and at football, and hope things work out for your dad."

"Yeah, I wish I could help him. He means well; he just doesn't get it, always pissed off at the world. He doesn't know how to talk to people, and since my mom left, I think he feels like he doesn't have anything to live for. They didn't have the best relationship, but at least it was something."

I called Jack feeling sorry for myself, and about Cindy, and my life at Bertram. What I didn't expect was to feel bad for him and his situation. It seems like football is the only positive thing in his life, and despite everything that is going on with him, he's there for me, willing to listen.

"Don't worry about things with Cindy," Jack replies.

"Thanks."

"Who do you guys play this week?"

"It's our first home game; we play Granger Academy. It should be interesting. We play our home games on Saturdays at two o'clock."

"Good luck, man. Get a big hit for me. We play Dunbar. Those kids are fast. Coach Murphy has put in a special defense to try to contain their quarterback, Christian Allen. Do you remember him in track last year? He ran the two hundred meters in like twenty-two seconds; he's only a junior. He's got a cannon for an arm. And their tailback, Trent Davis, won the state hundred meter final last year as a junior. They're undefeated."

"If you keep running the way you have been, you guys should be fine. Let me know how things are going with your dad and how things work out with Leigh."

"Yeah, you hang in there, too. Let me know how that new girl Taylor is. I'm out, Morris."

"Yeah, I'll catch up with you later."

I hang up the phone and watch the sun go down. I think about breaking up with Cindy, and I think about all the things that Jack is going through. Standing on that field, I feel completely lost and alone. I am detached from everything I have ever known. But at the same time, I feel fortunate to have a friend like Jack. His friendship is something I had always taken for granted, but now, I know how lucky I am.

CHAPTER 19

September 13

Saturday morning, I make my usual trek to the library to read the newspaper article about Unionville's Friday-night game.

THE DAYTON FLYER
High School Football: WEEK 3

The Unionville Rockets found themselves in a dogfight last night against a fast and strong Dayton Dunbar team. Unionville won the contest in double overtime, 28–21. Regulation ended in a 14–14 tie. Trent Davis led Dunbar with 180 yards rushing on only 20 carries. However, he was outdone by Jack Thompson who was the workhorse for Unionville, carrying the ball 35 times for 225 yards. His powerful running served the Rockets well in the overtime period, where Dunbar could not stop him. The 3–0 Rockets face Troy next week. Dunbar travels to Upper Arlington.

Every time I read about Unionville, it feels like a piece of me is missing. I'm supposed to be a part of that team. Thinking about Unionville makes it difficult to focus on the game I have to play today. And even though I know breaking up with Cindy was the right thing to do, I miss her already. And I miss being a part of a team where I know everybody. I miss being home.

After reading the article, I walk over to the cafeteria and see Kevin sitting by himself. After grabbing my breakfast, I ask Kevin if I can sit with him. At least he doesn't object to my sitting at his table.

"Unionville had a big win over Dunbar last night," I tell him.

Kevin looks me up and down and then lets out a deep breath. "They did? How did Iron City do last night?"

"They won 21–7 against Troy. Unionville plays Troy next week." I'm glad to bring Kevin good news, if it is good news.

"That's cool," Kevin says, sounding a bit more like his old self.

"Yeah, you excited about playing Granger today?"

"As much as I can be," Kevin replies. "I don't feel a part of this team."

"Listen, you have to let that go. Put it behind you. You have to focus on the game, or you're going to get hurt."

"Maybe I should quit," Kevin shoots back.

Shaking my head, I say, "Show these guys that you're better than that."

"You know, you're the only person I trust around here." Looking up at me, he says, "I'm sorry for yelling at you the other day. I know you tried to help."

"It's cool, man. Show these guys that we Dayton boys know how to play ball."

Kevin nods his head and says, "You know what, you're right."

We walk to the gym to grab our equipment and get ready for the game. I start my pregame ritual of walking the campus and doing some light stretching and running in the two acres of open space behind the locker room. In my football pants and my gray T-shirt with cut-off sleeves, I begin to put myself in the right frame of mind.

Back at the gym, the trainer is taping ankles, while some of the guys are stretching and getting loose. About two hours before the game, we jog out to the field house and begin our special team warm-up: kicking, punting, and throwing. I work with the punters, catching punts.

Within a half hour, the Granger team pulls up in its school bus. My heart begins to pound, and, already, I'm ready for the kickoff.

Terrance comes over to me and asks, "You nervous, Morris?"

"Naw," I lie. "I'm good."

"Cuz I am. I always get nervous before games. I used to let it bother me, until someone told me it was good to be a little bit nervous. It gets you sharp, ready to play."

I come clean and tell Terrance, "Honestly, I get so nervous before games. Sometimes, I feel like I'm going to throw up."

"Hey, Morris, it just means you're human. It's a good thing. It just means that you care. You just have to channel that energy and make it work for you." Terrance smiles. "You know, I've been meaning to tell you, ever since that little fight we got in, I got some respect for you. You know, you came here, not knowing anybody, kicking some ass. You're all good in my book."

I smile and say, "Yeah, you're not so bad yourself." I can only think that maybe I have made a friend in Terrance.

Kickoff is just ten minutes away when our first string nose guard goes down with a pulled calf muscle during warm-ups. He can't run. Coach Carlson tells Kevin he will be starting at nose guard. Determination fills Kevin's eyes—he will finally get his chance to prove himself to the team. He comes over and says, "I'm gonna stick somebody today."

Granger wins the coin toss and decides to receive. We line up our kickoff team. As the ball flies through the air, Kevin and I sprint down the field and destroy the blocking wedge, taking out the first two players. Kevin flies in and punishes the return man. Granger has no idea they are going to meet the pent-up frustration and rage of Kevin Gordon. He's in the huddle ... growling.

On the line of scrimmage, Kevin digs his cleats into the ground. The turf flies up behind him. On the first play, he does a swim technique over the center. It is a dive play to Granger's tailback. Kevin plants his helmet squarely on the chest of the unsuspecting running back. The force knocks the runner off the ground. He and Kevin are both airborne. The loud pop echoes through the stadium as Kevin drives the runner into the ground, as though he is trying to put him six feet under. The players on the defense go to congratulate him on his big hit, but he shrugs them off. He returns to the spot of the ball and calls for the defense to huddle up. Everyone just looks at each other. Kevin's eyes are glazed over. He's in a different place.

By the second quarter, Granger's center is shaking. Kevin spits on the ball and grunts. He has ten tackles, and they are some of the most violent hits I have ever seen. He's no longer the kid who got taped. He has created his own identity. He's a freaking animal, one whom nobody wants to mess with.

We pound Granger, 35–7. Terrance runs like a madman, scoring four touchdowns. Three of them are long runs. One is a seventy-three-yard punt return.

I record twelve tackles and an interception. While playing tailback, I see Taylor in the stands, and I want to show off for her. Late in the fourth quarter, I score a touchdown.

After the game, Coach Carlson brings the team together in the end zone. "Men," he begins, "great effort out there today. Rest up tomorrow. We have a light practice on Monday. Remember to get your schoolwork done. And don't forget to be on your best behavior." When I look over at Kevin, I see complete satisfaction on his face.

After the game, I see Taylor standing with a group of her friends. She makes her way through the crowd. I carry my helmet and shoulder pads. The eyeblack is smeared on my face. She comes up and gives me an unexpected kiss on the cheek. "Great game," she says. "Nice touchdown."

"I forgot how much I missed running the ball."

"Yeah, well, awesome job."

"It's nice to know I have someone in my corner."

"Well," Taylor laughs, "I'm your biggest fan."

On the way back to the gym, we take the long way around campus and talk. I know that I need to tell her about breaking up with Cindy. "So," I say, "I talked to Cindy this week."

"Oh," Taylor says.

"I told her that I thought it was best if we moved on. You know, stayed friends."

"How did she feel about that?" Taylor asks, moving closer to me.

"Well, I don't think that she was too excited about it, but I think she understands." I try to make it sound like things went better than they did.

"That must've been hard."

"You know, once it was over, it felt like a giant weight was lifted off my shoulders. It wasn't fair to either one of us. She has her life in Unionville."

"Well, it sounds like you made the right decision, especially if you feel better after talking to her."

Taylor and I continue to walk through the campus. The leaves have started to change color, and the smell of fall is in the air.

We complete the loop around campus, and Taylor walks me to the front door of the gym. She looks me in the eyes and takes my hands in hers. She smiles her perfect smile and says, "I know breaking it off with Cindy was tough, but I'm glad you did."

"Seriously?"

"Yeah, seriously."

I look at Taylor and say, "I'm glad I met you here."

Taylor puts her arms around me and pulls me close. She gives me a kiss on the lips. Her lips are soft and wet. Looking at me, she says, "Me, too."

CHAPTER 20

September 15

Mr. Tanner opens the cardboard box in the front of the room. Some students look on with anticipation, some with dread. No one knows what to expect. The books are black with an orange binding and green writing on the front.

"Mr. Morris, would you help me pass out our new books?" Mr. Tanner asks.

I jump to my feet like it's a football drill. In a short period of time, Mr. Tanner has earned my respect. As I pass out the books, I read the cover: *The Dharma Bums*, by Jack Kerouac. I've heard of Hemingway and Steinbeck, but Kerouac?

"Ladies and gentlemen, raise your hands if you have ever heard of the Beat Generation?" asks Mr. Tanner, smacking the novel into his hand.

No response.

"Allen Ginsberg?"

Silence.

"William S. Burroughs?"

Nope.

"*On the Road?*"

Still, no reply.

"Well," Mr. Tanner reflects, "it appears as though I have my work cut out for me. One of my favorite authors of all time is Jack Kerouac. He was a Beatnik. The Beat Generation was characterized by individuals who rebelled against contemporary society. Does anybody here feel that way?"

We all raise our hands.

He continues, "Allen Ginsberg was a famous poet and writer during the fifties. He is best-known for writing the famous poem *Howl*." Tanner pauses for effect and, from memory, begins reciting the first few lines of the poem.

Then he continues, "William S. Burroughs wrote *Naked Lunch* about his heroin addiction. The book was actually banned until court rulings said it could be published. Kerouac's most famous novel is *On the Road*. That novel covers his insane road trips from New York to California and back again with his best friend, Dean Moriarty. Kerouac lived the life: living free, hitchhiking, seeing the world, and then writing about it. I think that most of you will find that Kerouac will capture your attention. Zen Buddhism is one of his topics."

The class chuckles and looks at each other.

"Is that funny?" Mr. Tanner asks with a serious expression on his face.

"No," the class replies in unison.

"Good, because by the end of this week, we will be meditating like Kerouac and his traveling companion from the book, Japhy Ryder."

Meditating? Who is this guy? This is English class.

"I know what you're all thinking. Meditation?"

I look at Taylor, and we nod our heads in agreement.

"Just give it a chance. Kerouac will make you see the world in a different way. We will study the beat writers and Kerouac's life and his ultimate demise. He was a hero to many."

I don't know how Mr. Tanner does it, but when it comes to his class, I actually want to be here.

As the week passes, I look forward to our meditation day in English class almost as much as our football game on Friday night.

Mr. Tanner comes into class Friday morning with a blanket and some thin yoga mats. A student helps him carry them into the room. He passes the mats out, and everyone sits down around the room. Tanner explains how to sit in the lotus position, but he also explains that his bad knees prevent him from doing so. Some of the girls in the class demonstrate their flexibility.

"Very good," Mr. Tanner observes. "Now, if you can't sit in the lotus position, simply cross your legs like this. Now, take your thumb and pointer finger and touch them together."

Everyone in the class gets into the lotus position, or they cross their legs.

"Now, has anyone ever seen the movie the *Lion King?* Rafiki demonstrates the proper sitting position and hand position."

Everyone's hands shoot up, until we remember that it's a Disney film, and we quickly lower our hands.

"Nothing to be ashamed of," Tanner laughs. "That monkey has a deeper understanding of the world." In his best Rafiki imitation, he says, "Oh, the past can hurt."

The whole class laughs.

"Now, once you are sitting correctly, and your hands are in the right position, we are going to work on breathing and paying attention to our breath."

The class lets him take us on his little experiment.

"Mr. Morris, how still does Kerouac sit in the pages you read for homework last night?"

I sit up with pride. I haven't missed an assignment in Tanner's class since the first day of school. "He sat so still two mosquitoes landed on him and didn't even bite him."

"Mr. Morris, you did the reading. We have a Bodhisattva in class, an enlightened being. Good for you," Mr. Tanner comments with a wink. He continues, "With meditation, you can begin to quiet your mind. You will find a new ability to focus."

Mr. Tanner takes the class through an entire meditation. I sit and breathe and focus on my breath, trying to clear my mind by letting go of all my thoughts. At first, some kids laugh and joke around, but soon, they get into the meditation. A million thoughts pop into my head, everything from Taylor to Cindy to moving from

Unionville and starting my new life at Bertram. But after a while, I begin to feel my body relax and my mind clear. The almost immediate effects encourage me. After the meditation, Mr. Tanner starts throwing out information about the Four Noble Truths and the Eightfold Path. He talks about the fact that all life is suffering, but he tells us that that there is a way to end the suffering. He talks about enlightenment and moments of Satori. By the end of the class, I want to learn all about Zen Buddhism. As for having a quiet mind, I want that as well.

Mr. Tanner stops class and says, "For those of you who are athletes, you might find that meditation can help you with your athletic performance." He looks over at me and says, "I'm starting a meditation club on Wednesday nights from seven to eight. If you're interested, come and see me."

After class ends, I walk over to Mr. Tanner and say, "Mr. Tanner, I'd like to be a part of the meditation class."

Tanner smiles, puts his hand on my shoulder, and says, "I was hoping you would."

CHAPTER 21

September 16

I sit in my dorm reading *The Dharma Bums* when my phone rings. Without looking at the phone, I answer, "Hello?"

"Billy?" My mom's voice comes over the phone.

"Yeah, it's me."

"Hi, honey. It's Mom. I've been trying to get a hold of you."

"I've been busy," I say.

"Are you okay?" she asks.

"I'm doing fine," I answer shortly.

"Listen, I know you're not very happy with me right now, but I want you to know that this decision was not easy."

"Yeah, whatever."

"Billy, I want you to know that I love you. Bertram is a great opportunity for you."

"Mom, Bertram was a great opportunity for you to get rid of me. And it looks like things are working out fine … for you."

"You know that's not true. There are more opportunities at Bertram than you would ever have back in Unionville. I believe that with all my heart." She pauses. "How is school going anyway?"

I don't know how to answer her question. If I really think about it, my transfer to Bertram, although difficult, has been filled with some positive things: my first varsity football game, Mr. Tanner's English class, and, of course, Taylor.

"It's been okay, I guess. My crazy English teacher is all wrapped up in Buddhism. I got in a fight with the captain of the football team during practice, and my roommate was taped from head to toe with athletic tape."

My mom says, "At least you didn't say you were bored." She laughs on the other end of the line.

My mom always has a way of putting a good spin on things. I had forgotten that we used to be good friends. After my dad moved out, we were actually close. My sister, my mom, and I were brought together by the divorce. We became our own little team, determined to get through the mess.

"Yeah, well, I haven't been bored." I can feel my defensive wall crumbling under my mother's kind voice, as I start to consider that maybe her decision to send me to Bertram was one she really did think would help me in the long run. For the first time, I think that she might have had my best interest in mind.

"It sounds like you are doing some interesting things there. Richard and I are planning on coming to Cleveland for Thanksgiving. We'll come and spend some time, take you out to dinner."

"I'll be here. I've got nowhere else to go."

"It's good to hear your voice. I've been thinking about you. I was about to call the office and tell them I couldn't get a hold of you. I miss you."

"Yeah, it's good to talk to you."

"You're going to love South Carolina. The weather here is beautiful. It's nice to get out of dreary Unionville. Richard has found a great job, and I have gone on a couple of interviews. I may even go back to school. You know, I never did get to finish college, having your sister and all. I think it would be kinda fun to be a student again."

"You can take my place," I joke, lightening the mood.

My mom is silent for a moment. "Hey," she says, "let's make Sunday afternoon our talk time. I don't want to go so long without talking to you."

I promise to make Sunday our time to talk. Hanging up the phone, I'm glad that I finally got a chance to speak to my mom.

CHAPTER 22

September 17–October 28

During the next few weeks, our English class studies the Beat Generation, Zen Buddhism, and Jack Kerouac. On that first Wednesday night, I meet a small group of students, including Taylor, for a thirty-minute meditation led by Mr. Tanner. He keeps me after the meditation class on the first night.

"Mr. Morris, I want to commend you on your attendance tonight and your marked improvement in my class."

Looking down at the floor, I say, "I like coming to your class."

Mr. Tanner laughs. "Well, it sounds like a win-win situation. I thought you might be interested in meditation. I think you can benefit a great deal from it."

Nodding my head, I say, "I'm interested."

"Do you want to know why I learned meditation?" Tanner asks.

I shrug my shoulders. "Sure."

"When I returned from Vietnam, I was diagnosed with PTSD."

"What's that?" I ask.

"Post-traumatic stress disorder. I had bad anxiety attacks. The doctors wanted to put me on all this different medication. I had a friend who was Buddhist, and he suggested I try meditation first. I figured I had nothing to lose. He told me that meditation would help my anxiety and that the rest of my life would benefit. I couldn't get started soon enough. Because I was scared to death by the severity of my anxiety, I worked at meditation like my life depended on it, and in a lot of ways, it did."

"How long did it take until you started to feel better?"

"Well, let's just say Vietnam never really goes away, but at least I could handle my life. Meditation can make a difference, but you have to do your part. Would you be interested in enhancing your focus on the football field?"

"I'd like to learn."

Mr. Tanner explains, "You see, there's a thing called mental imagery. It's kind of like seeing plays on the football field before they happen. There's the power of the human mind. More often than not, if we focus our energy in the right way, we can predict the outcome of things in our lives before they happen to us."

I look at him and ask, "Mr. Tanner, why are you helping me?"

"Well, Mr. Morris, let's just say I know how it feels to be the new kid."

Wanting to ask Tanner a million questions, I simply say, "Thank you."

We cruise through our football schedule, winning week in and week out. Terrance Strong dominates on the football field. He runs like a machine, and our defense dominates. We end our regular season undefeated, with a perfect 9–0 record. We are ranked fourth in our region for Division II, and we are psyched for the playoffs.

I make it a point to go to the library study room every night and meditate for thirty minutes on my own. I'm amazed at how much quieter my mind is. I'm now better able to control my moods and emotions, and my ability to focus in class and on the football field improves.

But on Saturday after our final game, even though everyone else is celebrating with a pizza party in the cafeteria, I sit alone in my room. Even though I'm a part of the Bertram team, it still doesn't feel like my team. Pulling the newspaper clippings I've collected from Unionville's season out of my desk drawer, I spread them out across my desk. Leaning back in my chair, I rub my eyes, not sure how I should feel about missing out on their season. I study myself, my dark hair, my hazel eyes, in the mirror above my desk; I can see that I am no longer a kid. I'm a different person, and I'm proud of the person looking back at me. Looking down at my desk, I arrange the articles from Unionville's season, weeks four to ten, and reread each one:

THE DAYTON FLYER
High School Football: WEEK 4

Unionville extended its record to a perfect 4–0 by defeating and dominating the Troy Trojans by the score of 42–14. Jack Thompson continued to explode on the gridiron. He upped his rushing total to 810 yards by rushing for 170 yards and scoring five touchdowns against a struggling Troy team. Unionville's passing attack was again led by Danny Towers. Towers threw for over 300 yards. Troy scored both of its touchdowns late in the fourth quarter. Unionville hosts Xenia next Friday.

THE DAYTON FLYER
High School Football: WEEK 5

Unionville stayed undefeated at 5–0 by shutting out Xenia, 17–0. Jack Thompson ran for an even 200 yards and one touchdown. Kicker Jacob Conroy added a 35-yard field goal at the end of the half to put the Rockets up 10–0. Woody Fletcher demonstrated why he's a starting sophomore by adding an interception for a touchdown to clinch the victory for the Rockets. Unionville travels to Walnut Hills next week.

THE DAYTON FLYER
High School Football: WEEK 6

Unionville stands at 6–0. Walnut Hills boasted about its dynamic duo of tailback and fullback, Chris Snow and Tim Cage, but the Unionville defense shut them down. The explosive running game was led by Unionville's Jack Thompson, who ran for 164 yards and three touchdowns, as the Rockets ran away with a 35–17 victory. Danny Towers continued to demonstrate his skills by throwing for 318 yards and two touchdowns. Chris Snow and Tim Cage were held to 35 yards and 15 yards, respectively. Unionville heads to Westerville Central next Friday.

THE DAYTON FLYER
High School Football: WEEK 7

Unionville traveled to Columbus to play a tough Westerville Central team. Quarterback Danny Towers led the team with 285 yards passing and three touchdowns. Westerville was on the losing end of a 28–21 defeat. Sophomore cornerback Woody Fletcher iced the game when he intercepted a Westerville pass and returned it 70 yards for the game-winning touchdown late in the fourth quarter. Jack Thompson kept the Westerville defense honest with 214 yards on 33 carries. Unionville plays at Middletown next Friday.

THE DAYTON FLYER
High School Football: WEEK 8

Unionville toppled a tough Middletown team by a score of 14–10. Both touchdowns were scored by a hard-running Jack Thompson, who ran for 245 yards on 35 carries. Unionville fumbled four times inside the Middletown 20-yard line. Coach Mike Murphy attributed the turnovers to the torrential downpour of rain that persisted throughout the night. He was quoted as saying, "That field was a quagmire. I'm surprised there weren't more turnovers by both teams." Unionville travels to Hamilton next week.

THE DAYTON FLYER
High School Football: WEEK 9

Unionville defeated Hamilton by the final score, 49-7. Quarterback Danny Towers threw for five touchdowns and 325 yards. Hamilton was never in the game. Their only score came with two minutes left in the fourth quarter. Jack Thompson added two touchdowns and 188 yards on the ground to round out the scoring. Thompson led the defense with 15 tackles and an interception. Unionville hosts Cincinnati Xavier next Friday night as it attempts to post its first undefeated season in school history.

THE DAYTON FLYER
High School Football: WEEK 10

Unionville goes a perfect 10–0. Jack Thompson has made himself a candidate for Mr. Football in Ohio. In his last regular season game as a sophomore, he ran for 185 yards, putting him over the 2,000-yard mark. Unionville toppled a tough Cincinnati Xavier team by winning, 21–7. The humble Thompson was quoted as saying, "This is a team sport. I'm just glad that our team has the opportunity to go to the playoffs." Unionville will attempt to surpass its semifinal defeat last year by making it to the state championship game. This team will be one to be reckoned with.

Neatly stacking the articles, I put them back in my desk drawer and call Jack.

"Billy!" my best friend's voice echoes over the phone. It seems like forever since we last talked.

"Hey, man," I blurt out.

"What's up, bro?" Jack asks.

"Not much, just sitting here in my dorm looking over the newspaper articles of your undefeated season. Who would have thought? Jack Thompson, more than two thousand yards in just ten games. Dude, you're a monster."

"Yeah, man. It's been awesome. Can you believe an undefeated season? Everyone in the town is going nuts.

The funny thing is, I just want things to be normal. You know, things have been crazy around here."

"Why? What's up?"

Jack lets out a long sigh. "Leigh broke up with me. Says I'm out of control. She said she's had enough."

"Really?"

"Yeah, can you believe it? And to make matters worse, my dad got his second DUI this week."

"I thought he lost his license?"

"Yeah, that's just it. He got another one on a suspended license. The police made him do the sobriety test, walk the line, and say the alphabet. To top it off, it was after a game. The football bus passed my old man walking the line. All the seniors started busting on me, telling me my old man's a drunk. I flew out of my seat and punched Tolliger right in the mouth. The whole back of the bus broke out into a brawl. Coach Murphy had the driver pull over, and he made the whole team jog the back roads all the way to school."

"Man, I bet Murphy was pissed."

"I thought his head was going to explode. His face turned this dark shade of purple. We knew we were in trouble."

"Did everybody make it back to school?"

"Yeah, we made it," Jack says.

"I've been reading about you guys. It sounds like you've been tearing up the league."

"Football is my only outlet. My dad's driving me crazy. He comes home drunk, pissed off. Thursday night is dollar beer night at The Tavern. He comes home all liquored up and starts pushing me around, telling me how worthless I am. He usually throws a couple of punches until he passes out. So when it comes game time, I've got this anger inside me, and I have to get it out. It's like somebody turns a switch. When I put that helmet on, it's revenge time. Whoever we're playing pays for every punch and every insult my dad throws at me. Every time he tells me I'm nothing, stupid, weak, I feel like I'm going to fly into a rage. By the time Friday night rolls around, I don't even want to just play the other team. I want to kill 'em, make 'em pay. It's like I'm some possessed animal. I hit this one kid so hard, I broke his jaw, knocked some of his teeth out."

Jack sounds like a different person. With his mother gone, he really has nowhere to turn. I ask him, "What can I do to help?"

"You can get me the hell out of here before I snap. My old man has to go to court. He may have to go to jail. I don't know what I'm going to do. Right now he's out on bail and guess where he is?"

"The Tavern?"

"You got it," Jack says, sounding defeated.

"What are you going to do?"

"I don't know. It's tough. Pressure from the coaches, my old man, it's starting to wear on me. We have our first playoff game this Friday. The only thing that's getting me through this is football." He pauses. "And you. I feel better when I can talk to you and get some of this stuff off my chest."

"What about your mom?" I ask.

"Haven't heard from her."

"What does Coach Murphy have to say about all this?"

"He said he would help if I needed anything."

"What can I do?" I ask.

"Just be a friend."

When I hang up the phone, I think about my best friend. I think about the fact that no one should have to deal with the things he is dealing with. And to make it worse, he's by himself, and I feel like I'm on the other side of the world. I should be there. I should be there to help my friend.

CHAPTER 23

October 30

Mr. Tanner strolls into class with boxes filled with copies of our next novel. When he calls for my assistance in passing out the books, I jump from my seat. As I pass them out, I check out the cover. The cover of the novel is blue with a picture of an armadillo on the front. The title reads: *A Prayer for Owen Meany*, by John Irving. I wonder what could be better than Jack Kerouac. The book is more than five hundred pages. At Unionville, I had never even read a novel, let alone one this big.

Mr. Tanner pulls me aside and quietly says, "Once you get started, you won't be able to put it down."

Mr. Tanner addresses the class once all the books have been handed out. "Our newest author is John Irving. He has written some classic novels: *The Cider House Rules*, *The World According to Garp*, and *A Widow for One Year*. I think that you will find *A Prayer for Owen Meany* to be a great read."

We read part of the first chapter aloud. It's titled: "The Foul Ball." The chapter is completely confusing, and I wonder how I am going to get through the book.

Mr. Tanner says, "For those of you who are a bit confused, don't lose heart. We'll go over the readings in detail. Once you get it, the story really flows. Plus, it deals with some weighty issues: religion, best friends, and the death of loved ones, both the good and difficult things that life tends to throw at us and asks us to figure out."

I feel like Mr. Tanner is a mind reader, like he's talking directly to me. I decide to give the novel my best effort.

After class, I meet Taylor in the hall. "How are things going?" I ask.

"Great," she says, as she smiles her perfect smile. "Are you looking forward to the game this Friday?"

"Yeah, but I'm nervous. It's hard to believe that the playoffs are already here. All the seniors on the team act like it's no big deal."

"Well, all the students are really excited. The whole school is buzzing."

"Do you want to meet for lunch?" I suggest. "I need to talk to Mr. Tanner before my next class."

Taylor playfully pushes my shoulder. "I'll see you at lunch."

I walk up the stairs to Mr. Tanner's office. He's sitting at his desk reading Herman Melville's *Moby-Dick*. I knock, and he glances up and says, "Ah, Mr. Morris, do come in. What can I do for you?"

I don't know where to start, but it all just comes out, the whole story. I tell him about Unionville, my mom and Dick moving, Jack and his old man, Cindy, Taylor, and football.

Surprisingly, Mr. Tanner doesn't flinch. "Being a kid ain't easy," he says. "And, I have some news for you. Life isn't easy, and the sooner you figure that out, the better. All you can do is make the best of what you've got. And from here, it seems like you got a lot going for you. You're a strong, athletic kid, and you have a pretty good head on your shoulders. And from what I can tell, the best part about you is that you can be this tough-guy football player, but you have this whole other side to you that is about being caring and compassionate. And that might be your best quality."

I've never had anyone mention anything to me about my compassion.

"You know," he adds, "the thing I learned from Vietnam is that everything is temporary, even the bad stuff. The way I look at it is you don't have it so bad. You're at one of the best prep schools in the state, your football team is undefeated, and you're playing in your first playoff game this Friday night. From where I'm sitting, things could be a whole lot worse."

I agree with Mr. Tanner, but my worry and focus have shifted from my own problems to Jack's. I explain, "I feel helpless, like there's nothing I can do to help my friend. And the worst part of all of this is that I'm not there to help him."

"Your buddy Jack sounds pretty tough, cut from the same mold as you I imagine. I have a feeling he's going to be all right. The only things you can do now are the things that you *are* doing. Keep in touch with him. Let him know you're there for him. Let him know that you're his friend. I'm sure when you talk to him, you feel the same way."

It feels good to talk to Mr. Tanner, someone who understands things. He's not just a great teacher; he's a great friend.

I get up from the chair in Mr. Tanner's office and shake his hand. "Thanks for your help."

"Anytime," he says, "my door is always open."

A thick blanket of snow shrouds Bertram Academy. It collects high on the bare branches, and a welcome silence pervades the campus. The wind blows, and as I trudge to the cafeteria to meet Taylor, I contemplate the advice that Mr. Tanner gave me. He's right. Things could be a whole lot worse. I promise myself to do everything in my power to help Jack, and I hope that he'll be okay.

CHAPTER 24
October 31–November 2

The week before our first playoff game seems to drag, increasing my anxiety to unbearable levels. For once, I'm glad to have school to occupy my thoughts. All the students talk about the big game in the hallways, in classes, and at lunch. I can't escape "the game."

At practice, it's business as usual. The seniors don't seem as nervous as I am. Terrance Strong is as cool as they come; nothing bothers him, especially because he's preparing to announce where he's going to go to play college football. He has been the recruiting target of just about every major college: Ohio State, Michigan, USC, Florida State, and Miami. He takes it all in stride. During the season, Terrance got letters from all the major colleges. He's a celebrity at age seventeen.

After practice on Tuesday, Terrance sees me in the locker room. "Hey, Morris. What's up?"

"Not much," I say, splashing some water on my face. "Just a little nervous for the game."

"Yeah, I know. I felt the same way my sophomore year." Terrance fixes his hair in the mirror. "Everything seemed so new, but once you put that helmet on, get on that field, all that melts away. You're in the zone; nothing's going to bother you there."

I have to agree. Once the game starts and that helmet is on, there is nothing that I can't do. I make a complete transformation. Talking to Terrance about the game makes me feel better.

"Hey, what are you going to do about schools? Have you decided?" Immediately, I feel like I've crossed the line into his business.

Terrance glances over at me. "Yeah, I think I made up my mind. It's been a tough decision, you know. Lots of people making lots of promises." He pauses and looks at me through my reflection in the mirror. "Why? What do you think? Where do you think I should go? What would you do?"

Was Terrance asking my opinion? "Well," I begin cautiously, "it's always been my dream to play at Ohio State, but any Division I school would be awesome."

Terrance smiles, but he doesn't give away the secret. He will save that for Thursday evening when he announces where he is going to college to play ball.

Thursday night, Terrance is dressed up like he's going to meet the president or something. He wears a black suit, a bright-red tie, and shined black-leather shoes.

Bertram's student body and just about every sports reporter in Ohio greet him at the press conference.

Terrance sits at a long table in front of the auditorium and talks into the microphone. "I just want to thank some people. First, I have to thank my mom and my dad." He looks over at his parents and nods his head. "I want to thank my coaches and my teammates. They made all this possible."

He thanks just about everybody on the planet.

He reads his comments from a sheet of paper. "This decision has been the hardest one in my life. I want to thank everyone for their support." When he gets to the bottom of the page, he looks out over the crowd and takes a deep breath. In front of him on the table are three hats: Michigan, Ohio State, and USC. Terrance reaches down and picks up the Ohio State hat and adjusts it on his head. Smiling, he says, "I'm going back home to Columbus. I will be playing football at The Ohio State University."

Everybody claps and cheers.

Terrance stands up and hugs his mother and father, who look like the proudest parents in the world. Like a pro already, he heads over to the reporters and begins to answer questions.

CHAPTER 25

November 7

When we board the school bus and begin the one-hour ride to what the state calls a mutual site, the nerves begin to set in. The bus is quiet; everyone understands the gravity of our first playoff game. I sit next to Kevin with my headphones on, listening to my *pregame playlist*. I think about Jack and Unionville. They also have their first playoff game tonight. I talked to Jack after Terrance's announcement and told him what a huge production it was. Jack couldn't believe it. He said that maybe one day we could have a press conference and tell everybody where we wanted to go to school to play ball.

On the bus ride, I think about all the hype that comes with a first playoff game. All week, reporters, photographers, and cameramen were at our school during practice, interviewing the coaches and some of the players. Coach Carlson is constantly warning us about getting caught up in the excitement of people telling us how great we are, and how sometimes we might start to believe them. He warns, "If you get caught up in what everybody is saying, you lose focus. Losing focus loses ball games."

Before we leave for the game, I read a newspaper article about the team we are playing, the Springfield

Raiders. Springfield, just outside of Toledo, is a town like Unionville. The article describes how all the players are best friends, how they can't wait for the opportunity to play in the state playoffs. Coach Carlson, who I'm sure has watched hours of film on Springfield, is quoted as saying, "They are a great team with lots of good players at the skill positions, and their quarterback is a jitterbug who has a cannon for an arm."

The words stick in my head. How are we going to stop a quarterback with a cannon for an arm? And, more importantly, does our team share the same kind of comradery that Springfield has? All those kids grew up together; they are probably great friends. They want to win, not just for themselves, but for each other.

When we finally get to the field, the brakes on the bus squeal, and the doors swing open. Coach Carlson stands up, and everyone falls silent. "This is it, guys. Let's get focused and pull it together. Let's get it going!"

Everybody files off the bus, grabs their shoulder pads and helmets from the equipment van, and heads to the locker room. The mood is somber. Something is missing; the lack of energy is noticeable. Maybe the playoffs are old hat for the seniors, but not for me. I can barely keep myself together.

Coach Carlson calls the team together and gives his pep talk, but I can't concentrate on what he's saying. Because I'm so focused on the game, it just looks like his mouth is moving. We recite the Lord's Prayer and move out to the field, two hundred yards away. I can't wait for the game to start.

On the walk over to the field, I hear the band playing and drums pounding, like some Native American ritual. I feel like I've been thrown back in time, and this is some ancient warrior right of passage. The stands are dotted with gray and mostly red sweatshirts on the Bertram side; the pep bus has brought students from the Bertram campus. The other side of the bleachers is filled with the entire Springfield community. I imagine the town of Springfield as being empty tonight. Their side of the bleachers is a sea of purple and black, and fans pour out onto the track that surrounds the field. They carry signs that read: Purple People Eaters. My heart pounds as we walk through the gates and over the track. Sliding on my helmet and snapping on my chinstrap, I prepare for battle.

The Springfield Raiders wear black jerseys with purple numbers and purple pants. They all have long hair hanging out of the backs of their helmets. These kids are good old farm boys. Sloppy strong. And after the kickoff and my first contact of the game, I learn that they love to hit.

Maybe because Bertram won the state championship last year, everyone assumes that the competition will lie down, but it's just the opposite. Springfield is out for blood. They come out throwing better, running faster, and hitting harder than any team we have faced all year. They score on a long bomb and end a long drive with a short three-yard run. And for the first time all season, we're losing at halftime. With our second quarter field goal and their missed extra point after the second touchdown, the "Purple People Eaters" are up, 13-3. We're in a dogfight.

Terrance Strong speaks up at halftime before the coaches get into the locker room. *"Everybody wake up!"* He moves around the locker room, getting into everyone's face. *"What are we doing out there?"* He slams his helmet against a locker. "We've got one half to make this right, or our season is over. Is that what you want? *Is that what you want?"* With a crazed look in his eyes, he says, "Let's go! *We ain't done yet!"*

As Terrance finishes his rant, the coaches move into the locker room in a much calmer fashion. They break the team up into position meetings, trying to get everybody together to figure out how to win the game. They draw Xs and Os on the chalkboards, and they ask us why certain plays aren't working. Everything the coaches do at halftime prepares us for the second half, but Terrance's words wake us up.

With a feeling of desperation, we charge the field for the second half. I think Springfield is surprised when the third quarter starts. Our hitting, which was ferocious in the first half, elevates to an even greater intensity. On a sweep play, Marcus and I meet their tailback head-on. We drive through him and force him out of bounds. The running back groans as we crush him into the ground. Everyone on the Bertram sideline cheers and congratulates us. We jump to our feet, give each other high fives, and sprint back to the huddle, ready for more.

In the second half, bodies are flying everywhere. It's nasty and intense, and I love it. My nervousness subsides, and I feel like my focus is back. I use what I learned from Mr. Tanner about meditation to calm myself down. I'm in the zone.

Terrance takes some of his own advice and puts on a running display in the third quarter. Unfortunately, two turnovers: a fumble and an interception, keep the score: Springfield 13, Bertram 3.

In the fourth quarter, Terrance finally breaks one open. Springfield has contained him for three full quarters, but he breaks some long runs in the fourth. On a sweep to the right, he explodes through a tackle and slips around the right end. He's off to the races. His shoulders swing from side to side as he runs for a fifty-two-yard touchdown. The Bertram fans go crazy. The score is now, 13-9. Our kicker comes in for the extra point. The snap is fumbled by the holder, Mike Giffin, who tries to position the ball. He barely gets the ball set in time, and our kicker boots it through the uprights. We are down by three points with only five minutes to go in the game, 13-10.

On the kickoff, Springfield returns the ball to their thirty-five-yard line. Coach Kaplan pulls the defense together and shouts, "We need the ball back, fast. This is it, guys. You must play as much with your head as your heart. Don't quit. Don't give up. We can win the game."

We sprint out to Springfield's thirty-five-yard line and huddle up. On the first play, Springfield runs a dive play to their tailback over the right tackle. Kevin slants right into the play and puts a solid hit on the tailback, just as he is getting the handoff from the quarterback. Marcus sticks the ball carrier from his linebacker position. He rips the ball free, and Kevin jumps on the fumble. We have possession with less than five minutes in the game, deep in Springfield's territory.

Terrance is a marked man. Springfield knows he's going to get the ball. The question is whether their defense can stop him. On the first play, Terrance runs another sweep to the wide side of the field. He tries to get to the corner, but the cornerback has been playing solid all night. He comes up and wraps up Terrance. The Bertram fans groan, and I feel victory slipping from our hands. Coach Carlson tries a fullback trap on the next play. Sammy Jones never gets a good handle on it, and the ball comes loose. There is a mad scramble for the ball. Bodies fly everywhere, trying to recover the fumble. Somehow, Mike Giffin recovers the ball under a heap of bodies.

Coach Carlson calls a time out after he recovers from his near heart attack. He brings the team together and tries to calm us down, as he explains the importance of executing the next play.

"Listen," he begins, "the ball is on the left hash. Terrance's touchdown at the beginning of the fourth quarter was around the right end. That corner will not let that happen again. He'll run up like gangbusters. We must sell the run. *We must sell the run.*" With that, everyone knows where he's going. "We're gonna run the halfback pass. That corner will bite, and hopefully so will the safety." He looks at our wide receiver, Ryan Jackson. "Ryan, block your man for a count of three, then slide off him and get your butt in the end zone. Men, this is your time. This is your game. Make it happen."

The offense breaks the huddle and sprints onto the field. The stadium that was rocking with noise becomes strangely quiet. The play moves in slow motion as Mike Giffin takes the snap and pitches the ball wide to Terrance. Standing on the sideline, I see the corner read the sweep. He gets off Ryan's block and breaks toward Terrance. When Terrance brings the ball up like he is going to throw, the cornerback's eyes widen. He, and the safety, committed too soon. Ryan is wide open in the end zone. All Terrance has to do is get the ball to him. Terrance reaches back and lets the ball go. It wobbles end over end. The backside safety sprints toward Ryan, but Ryan is so wide open, even though the pass isn't perfect, he still catches it. Touchdown! The crowd goes wild, pulling me out of my trance. We are up, 16–13. We kick the extra point to make the score, 17-13, but three minutes still remain in the game.

We kick off deep to Springfield's ten-yard line. Their return man breaks a tackle and carries the ball all the way to their forty-five yard line. Two minutes and fifty seconds are left on the clock. Marcus calls a man-to-man defense, which we rarely play. The man-to-man defense has me locked on the opposing tight end. On the first play from scrimmage, Springfield's quarterback fakes a handoff to their tailback. I bite on the fake, and my man, the tight end, runs wide open across the field. The jitterbug with a gun for an arm hits him with a pass in perfect stride. Sprinting down the sideline, I start to close the gap as the tight end nears the end zone. Somehow, forty-five yards later, I literally jump onto his back around the twelve-yard line and drive him into the ground on our seven-yard line. All I can think is that my mistake just cost us the game.

Terrance comes over to me and shouts above the roar of the crowd. *"It's over. It's over. Can't let that play ruin the next one. Keep your head up. We need you."*

One minute and forty-five seconds remain in the game. It's Springfield's ball—first and goal. On the first play, they run a sweep to the right. Their linemen pull to the right in perfect unison. They drive and cut block our defensive linemen, but that frees up Marcus. He shoots through the line like a bolt of lightning and takes down the running back, making the stop.

One minute is left on the clock. On second down, the quarterback takes a fast three-step drop and throws a quick slant pass. The ball is low, and the receiver dives for it. The ball skips off the grass into the arms of the Springfield receiver who is on the ground, but the referee, who is blocked by all the bodies, signals that it is complete. He spins his arm to indicate to keep the clock running.

The entire defense jumps in the referee's face pleading our case.

"Incomplete! Incomplete!" I shout. "That wasn't even close. You couldn't even see that play!"

The referee looks at me. "Son," he shouts over the boos from the crowd, "watch yourself, or you'll be out of the game."

Marcus grabs me by the shoulder pads and pulls me back toward the huddle. "Don't be stupid, man! Keep your head about you."

I walk backward to the huddle facing the referee, who I can see is just waiting for me to open my mouth. The clock continues to run. Less than thirty seconds remain.

It's third and goal from the three-yard line. The quarterback drops back. Their wide receiver makes a great inside move on our corner, like the slant route, and our cornerback bites on the fake. The receiver breaks back outside to the corner of the end zone. He's wide open. The quarterback pauses, seeing his receiver so wide open; he wants to make the perfect pass. He pulls back and floats the ball toward the corner of the end zone. Just as the ball is about to land in the receiver's outstretched hands, Terrance, from his safety position, knocks the ball to the ground. The quarterback's moment of hesitation costs him the completion. We sprint over to Terrance and give him high fives. He's more relieved than excited.

With only ten seconds on the clock, Springfield's coach calls time out. It's fourth down. Coach Kaplan jogs out onto the field with his headset around his neck. He comes into the defensive huddle and somehow seems calm. "Last play, guys. Step up. You can do this. Even though they're on the three-yard line, they may try to throw. Their quarterback is their best player. I wouldn't be surprised if they put the game in his hands. *Let's go!*" He jogs back to the sideline. Marcus calls the defense, a regular 52 with man-to-man coverage on the receivers. I will not be fooled again.

The referee blows his whistle, and Springfield hustles to the line of scrimmage. Marcus and I call out the defensive signals: "Lion, Lion, Stick 44, Lion."

Above the roar of the crowd, their quarterback shouts, "Black 18. Black 18. Set, hut, hut." He takes the snap and rolls out to his right.

Coach Kaplan guessed right. Springfield put the game in the hands of their quarterback. He scrambles back and forth, and I mirror him from my linebacker position, slowly drifting into the end zone while keeping my man in my sight. The tight end hooks in behind me and sits in the back of the end zone. Suddenly, everything stops. My eyes meet the eyes of their quarterback. He releases the ball in a perfect spiral—only it comes in my direction. I step to my right and intercept the ball six yards deep in our own end zone.

My first reaction is complete surprise; my second reaction is to run like hell. I sprint toward the left sideline. The receiver runs at me full speed from the corner of the end zone, but I don't see the quarterback, who takes a direct course at my right knee. He dives in toward the ligaments in my knee, hoping to get me back for the interception, and chops my knees out from under me.

Still in slow motion, I spin in a complete circle in the air and land hard.

When I jump to my feet, real time resumes, and I'm smothered by the entire defense. They shout, "Way to go, man! You did it!"

The parents and students go crazy in the stands. We win the game, and I am the hero. The celebration begins.

CHAPTER 26

November 8

I'm dying to know how Unionville did in its first playoff game. I tried calling Jack on his cell last night, but all I got was his voicemail. When I get to the library, I hold my breath as I spread the paper out on the table and scan the sports page to read about Unionville's first playoff game.

THE DAYTON FLYER
High School Football—PLAYOFF WEEK 1

The Unionville Rockets started their playoff odyssey against the Zanesville Blue Devils last night. The Rockets came out throwing the ball using their powerful tailback, Jack Thompson, as a decoy. Quarterback Danny Towers threw all over Zanesville. His accurate passes punctured the Blue Devils' defense. After establishing a 28-point half-time lead, the Rockets gave the ball to Thompson, who punished the Zanesville defenders. He had 28 carries for 120 yards. Most of his yards and his only touchdown came in the second half. The Unionville defense was led by sophomore Woody Fletcher, who had two interceptions. Zanesville's Lionel Smith scored a touchdown late in the fourth quarter, but Unionville won, 35–7. The Rockets will face New Albany next Friday night at Dayton's Welcome Stadium.

I look up from the newspaper and see Taylor standing directly in front of me, wearing her usual Saturday-morning attire of sweatpants, sweatshirt, and baseball hat. There's something about her eyes, their comfort, and their acceptance, that makes me feel like I am home.

"I knew you'd be here," she says, sitting down next to me.

"Yeah, I had to check up on Unionville."

Taylor studies my face. "So ... what was the score?"

"Thirty-five to seven, they won. Their quarterback threw for three touchdowns."

Taylor looks like she's impressed. "How did your friend Jack do?"

"One hundred twenty yards rushing and a touchdown."

"Wow, not a bad night."

"Yep," I say, feeling empty inside.

"So then what's the matter? Why do you look so down?" Taylor asks.

I shake my head. "It's nothing."

"After your game last night, I figured you'd be excited."

"I guess it's cool and all playing in the playoffs with *the* Terrance Strong, but it's not the same. Playing for Unionville was different. The guys here are good guys, but it's not even close to playing with the friends you grew up with. I want to be playing with them."

"I know you're frustrated, but did you hear the Bertram fans last night? After you made that interception, everyone was yelling, 'Who was that? Where did that kid come from?' It was awesome. You were the man; you were the hero. I was so excited for you, and not because of the interception. I was proud of you, because all I could think about were the things you've overcome to get to this point, to make that kind of difference in so many people's lives."

Taylor really makes me think. I've had to prove myself over and over, and I've had to do it away from my friends and my family. "Thanks a lot," I say.

Taylor gets this look like she's considering an important question. "You can thank me by coming to the school play."

"I wouldn't miss it. When is it?" I ask.

"Thursday night," Taylor says with a hope-filled look.

I give her the thumbs up. "It's a deal."

"It's Shakespeare, but it's a comedy. I think you might like it," Taylor says, trying to convince me, even though she doesn't need to.

"If you're in it, I can't see why I wouldn't."

"It's about love at first sight, and then there's some confusion, but it all works out in the end."

"Sounds like my life," I mumble under my breath.

"What?" Taylor asks.

"Nothing." I look around the library, making sure the coast is clear. I lean toward her and put my hands on her lower back, touching her skin under her sweatshirt. She leans into me, and her fingers rub the back of my neck. She pulls me to her, and we kiss for a long minute. The kiss is everything I thought it would be. I don't want to let her go. Eventually, we separate and look at each other, at a loss for words.

Taylor finally says, "Wow. That was really ... nice."

I just nod my head because I can't find the words.

"So, I, um, have play practice tonight. So, I guess I'll see you tomorrow?"

"Okay," I say, barely able to speak.

Taylor gives me a hug, and I kiss her again. The feeling that I get is like—well, it's like everything in the world makes sense. Being with Taylor just feels right.

She walks out of the library, and I sit on the chair at the far end of the library, thinking. Three months ago, I thought my life was over and that I was going to lose touch with all of my friends. I felt more afraid than I thought I ever could be. Since then, I have made a game-saving interception and met the coolest girl ever. But still, I feel torn between two worlds: Bertram and Unionville.

On Sunday night, I get a phone call. "Hello?" I answer.

"Hi, honey. How have you been?" my mother asks.

How can I explain to her that I made a game-saving interception, met the girl of my dreams, and found an English teacher who has changed my life? How can I explain to her that I don't know how I feel, how I miss my friends back in Unionville? Where should I start? I say, "Things here are ... different."

"Different is good, I guess," my mom chuckles. "Hey, I really miss you, and I've been thinking a lot about you. I've been reading the paper and following your football season. Both Bertram and Unionville are undefeated. That's exciting. I can't believe there's a chance that you might play each other. Richard and I are planning to come to Cleveland. We could come for a game. I would love to see you."

"Yeah, I guess that would be fine," I answer. Part of me is excited to see my mom, but the other part is still angry with her. I resent that she left me on Bertram's doorstep, and now after all my hard work, she is just going to show up. It's not fair. She doesn't deserve to be a part of this season. Plus, I dread the thought of Dick giving me pointers on how to play the game.

"Well, that settles it. We will make our way up so we can see you play."

"Yeah, if we make it that far," I respond half-heartedly.

"Oh, don't be silly. Of course you guys are going to make it. By the way," my mother redirects the conversations, "have you talked to Cindy?"

It seems like forever since I thought about Cindy. Four months ago, we talked about staying together after high school. Now after coming to Bertram and meeting Taylor, my world has been turned upside down. I'm not sure where to begin, so I tell her, "I haven't really talked to Cindy. We kinda broke up."

"Broke up? Well, don't lose heart," my mom says. "I'm sure there are plenty of girls there who are probably just too shy to talk to the star of the football team."

"I'm not the star of the team, mom."

"That's not what I've been reading."

"What have you been reading down in South Carolina?" I ask.

"Oh, it's on the school's website. Bertram keeps it pretty well updated, especially with the team in the playoffs."

"And how do you know about Unionville?" I ask suspiciously.

"A friend from back home has been sending me clippings from the newspaper about all the games."

"What friend?" I ask.

"Just an old friend from the Paper Factory." My mother sounds reluctant to give me any more details. "Billy, I want you to know that I love you. I've been thinking about you every day. Good luck in your game this week. We'll be there soon. I can't wait to see you."

"I'll see you soon," I reply.

I hang up and stare out the window, thinking about what my mom had said. I think about the possibility of playing Unionville in the state championship game. My heart skips a beat. My whole life, I have anticipated playing on the same team with all my friends, and now just the opposite could happen. I might face my best friends on the biggest stage in high school sports. I wanted to make it to state with my friends, but I didn't want it to happen this way.

CHAPTER 27

November 9

I t's early Monday morning, and Mr. Tanner gets me thinking again when he says, "Faith and doubt often collide when it comes to religion, especially when there's no hard-core evidence that God exists."

The classroom is silent.

I pull out *A Prayer for Owen Meany* and run my finger over the cover, curious to find out what happens next. Funny enough, I really do want to know.

Mr. Tanner looks around the room as students flip through the pages of the book. "The concepts of fate and destiny have been around for as long as humans have. They've been in literature since Beowulf. We'll talk about Beowulf and Grendel later," he says, as he smiles, knowing what awaits us. "I love this book for one simple reason. It's about the roles that we play in other people's lives. We have the ability to influence people in such profound ways, life-changing ways. In this way, we are all instruments of God. Everything we do and say, no matter how big or small, affects the people whom we meet on a daily basis. If our intentions are good, we all can make a positive difference in the world. Ralph Waldo Emerson once said that success is about making people's lives better. Sometimes we can do that by being a good friend or helping someone in need. Sometimes, it's as simple as making a phone call." He glances in my direction.

We take a short quiz over the first few chapters. The book is slow at first, with too much background, but Mr. Tanner promises that the action will pick up and that the book will be worthwhile. At the end of the class, we finish our discussion. Tanner closes his book and sets it down on the desk that he sits on. He rocks forward on his hands and says, "This is one of my favorite novels. It has great characters. It's hilarious, but, most importantly, it's about friendship, the sacrifices friends make for each other. I may go so far as to say that true friendship, a really good friend, could be the most important thing in the world."

Jack Thompson, of all my Unionville friends, is the one who made sure to call me, to make me feel better when my mother decided to send me to Bertram. He is the one who, despite everything he has been dealing with at home, made a point of checking to make sure I was okay. He is the most important friend in my world.

On Thursday night, I'm relieved to have something other than the game to focus on. I put on a pair of brown corduroy pants, a powder-blue button-down shirt, and my leather jacket to walk across the already-dark campus. On my way to see my first play, I hear the buzz of the iron street lamps that line the walkway from the dorms to the auditorium. The newly shoveled sidewalk glistens, and salt crunches under my shoes. I look out into the woods that surround the campus. Snowflakes fall softly in front of the lights, and each tree branch bends under the snow's weight. It's a silence I never knew in Unionville.

Entering the auditorium, I find a seat and sit in the back row and read the program: The Bertram Academy Theater Presents: William Shakespeare's *Much Ado About Nothing*. The auditorium lights go down as the stage lights go up. When the play starts, a man runs into the center of the stage to announce that a bunch of people are returning from battle. He throws out names like Don Pedro, Claudio, Benedick, and Don John. I'm confused by the beginning of the play, but none of that matters when the next scene begins and Taylor has her first big part. She is one of the lead characters: Hero, the daughter of the town's governor. That part, I understand.

Taylor reinvents herself in so many ways: musician, singer, actress, and athlete. And then Mr. Tanner's words about friendship and fate hit me again. Taylor has come into my life and affected me like no one else. She is talented and smart, but above and beyond that, she is a great friend.

So here I am in the auditorium, and unbelievably, liking Shakespeare. I'm laughing and smiling, enjoying Taylor's performance. She brings her character to life. When the play ends, all the actors stand at the front of the stage to take a bow. The audience claps wildly, and

Taylor smiles her All-American smile. All I can think is that I have found the most amazing girl.

I meet Taylor after the play and say, "Hey, great job tonight. I'm really proud of you." Saying nice things is something that Taylor has taught me. I have never been good at communicating feelings like that, but she does so freely. I've learned that showing you are proud of someone is really important.

"Thanks for coming. I'm glad you made it." She gives me a big hug and introduces me to the other cast members. I recognize some of them from around school and in my classes, but I have never really met them. It's cool to meet a whole new group of people. There's a pizza party after the play with all the actors and stagehands. I actually meet a couple of really nice people. Jack would get a kick out of this—me hanging out with a bunch of actors.

In the middle of the party, Taylor walks over to me while I'm talking to my newest acting friend and says, "C'mon, let's get out of here."

Heading out the door of the auditorium, I ask Taylor, "Can I walk you back to your dorm?"

Taylor smiles and says, "I was kinda hoping you would." We hear chattering voices from the people on the snowy walkway. Taylor asks, "So, what did you think?"

I reach for her hand. "Honestly, I didn't think I was going to like it, but it was really, really good. You were awesome. It was funny, too. I never thought in a million years that I would like a play, especially Shakespeare, but maybe I just liked it because you were in it."

"You're too sweet." Taylor looks at me and takes my hand in hers.

"I actually laughed out loud. Dogberry and Verges were hilarious. I always thought Shakespeare was dark and violent—you know, death and insanity and all that."

"He wrote some dark stuff, but he also wrote great comedies. I love the part where Claudio and Don Pedro are tricked by Don John."

"That scene was great. Those actors actually became those other people."

"They all want to be professional actors. They take it very seriously. It's their passion, kinda like how you play football. Bertram has an excellent drama department. Maybe you should try out for the spring play?"

"Who, me? No way. I would embarrass myself. I think I'll stick to running track."

"Suit yourself, but I think you'd be fantastic."

I want the walk to last forever, but we soon arrive at her dorm. Taylor turns and looks at me and says, "Do you want to come in for a minute? My roommate went home for the weekend." My knees get weak. My heart starts racing, or it stops. I can't tell which. She leans into me and kisses me on the cheek. "Come on in. Curfew isn't for another forty-five minutes."

"Yeah, okay." I follow her to her second-floor room. She opens the door and turns on the light. Her room is a lot neater than mine. It actually smells good, too. She moves across the room and turns on her iPod. The song playing is "Sugar Mountain." She explains who Neil Young is, how he was her dad's favorite singer while she was growing up, how the song makes her feel safe. I listen to the music, and I am hooked. The strum of the guitar and cry of the harmonica put me on Sugar Mountain, wherever it is. I look at Taylor, and without a doubt, I know I am in love.

She walks over to her bed and sits down. She pats the area next to her, suggesting that I come and sit down.

I point to the bed and then to myself, making a "Who, me?" gesture. She shakes her head and rolls her eyes.

I walk slowly over to her bed and sit down beside her. Almost in the same motion, she leans over and kisses my lips. Her tongue lightly caresses my tongue, and we kiss like I have never kissed before. It's tender and passionate. I bring her close to me and hold her. We fall back onto the pillows and look into each other's eyes and laugh.

"I've wanted to do that since the first day I saw you," she says.

"Me, too," I agree.

As we listen to the rest of the playlist, each song gets ingrained in my mind. On this night, my heart is open, completely vulnerable. The possibility of doing more than kissing Taylor is on my mind, but it occurs to me that just being there, holding Taylor in my arms, is the best thing in the world.

"Do you want to know why I came to Bertram?" she asks.

"Sure, if you want to tell me."

"My mom and dad got divorced last year, and my mom had a really tough time. She kind of had, like, a nervous breakdown. After my dad left, I guess she couldn't handle it. We don't have a lot of money, so my mom applied for the scholarships at Bertram."

"You seem to be dealing pretty well with all that. You sure don't let it show."

"I guess that's why I like my music and acting so much. It's my way to escape. I put all my emotions in those things. When I'm on stage, playing my violin or acting out another person's life, I don't have to think about all the things in my own life. I love playing the violin. I get lost in the music. I go to a different place."

"I know what you mean. It's like football for me. When I put on that helmet, I know nothing can hurt me. It's the only place where I feel like I have control. It's like it's my world. You know, it's weird. I guess everybody has something they have to deal with. Nobody's got it easy."

"It's horrible, isn't it?" Taylor says.

"Horrible ... and great. Since I've come to Bertram, I've changed a lot, and I'm starting to like who I am. I like how I came here and earned a position on this team, how I told myself that nothing was going to keep me down. I think the bad stuff, the hard stuff, makes you better, stronger."

"Yeah, I guess I never really looked at it that way," Taylor says.

"I've really changed a lot."

Taylor looks around her room. "You know, when I first met you, I thought you were just a jock."

"Yeah, so what changed?"

Taylor shrugs her shoulders. "I don't know. It's just something about you. You're not like the rest. When I look in your eyes, I don't see that kind of person. I see something different. I see someone who cares about people, his friends, and his team. Someone who cares about me."

"You've helped me a lot since I got here."

"You've done the same for me." Taylor holds my hand.

"You've come to my games and helped me with school."

"What about you? Coming to my recitals, my games, and the play," she says.

"I wouldn't have missed it for the world."

Taylor looks over at her clock. "I hate to say it, but it's getting close to curfew. You'd better go."

She walks me to the door, but before she opens it, she kisses me on the lips. Her hand caresses the back of my neck, and my whole body tingles. I lean into her body and can feel her against me. She lets go of me and opens the door. Reluctantly, I walk out into the hallway.

"I'll see you tomorrow," she says, as she closes the door behind me.

On the way to my dorm, large snowflakes are falling. I breathe in the crisp, winter air and think about Taylor. And I think about the fact that I've never felt this way before.

CHAPTER 28

November 14

The snow comes down and sticks to the turf, while the maintenance crew from Canton's Fawcett Stadium shovels the snow off the field. The stadium, right next to the Pro Football Hall of Fame, is filled to capacity for the state semifinal playoff game.

Jogging on the field, I notice our stands are blanketed with our team colors: red, black, and gray. The other side of the stands is filled with the energized fans of the Wooster High School Generals. Terrance slaps me on the shoulder pads and says, "Let's get going, Morris."

Coach Kaplan huddles the defense and begins his pregame speech. "Keep focused on the game." The roar of the crowd forces him to shout his instructions, but in our huddled world, we are completely engaged. "Play every play until the whistle blows!"

We win the coin toss and decide to receive the kickoff. Because of the bad weather, the kick doesn't go far. Terrance catches it at our own thirty-five yard line, breaks a couple of tackles, and brings it back to Wooster's forty-yard line. We have great field position. Because of the giant gusts of wind, Terrance is put to work. I watch from the sidelines as Coach Carlson sends in dives and sweeps. Terrance busts through the line of scrimmage as our line opens huge holes. He puts deceptive moves on the defensive backs and pushes closer and closer to the end zone. On third and two, Terrance takes a handoff from Mike Giffin. As he reaches the first-down marker, he seems to relax and stand up. From his blind side, a 230-pound linebacker drives his helmet into the side of Terrance's head, and he goes down limply. Coach Carlson and our trainer sprint onto the field.

From the sideline, all I can see are Coach and the trainer. The entire stadium is quiet, fearing the worst. But, then I see Terrance's legs shift from side to side. This is a sign that at least he's okay. After about ten minutes, they help him to his feet, each grabbing an arm. Terrance wobbles back and forth. They take him to the bench, where he complains that he's seeing double and that everything is blurry.

What are we going to do? I think to myself. Losing Terrance means ... but before I can finish my thought, Coach Carlson looks directly at me and says, "Morris, get in there for Strong. We're going to run I left 39 pitch. Tell Tommy to get out there on the sweep. If he can get to their outside linebacker, you're in for a touchdown."

"Okay, Coach," I say, as I start toward the huddle.

Coach Carlson grabs me by the back of my shoulder pads and spins me around to face him. He's calm and confident. "Son, there's no reason you can't do this. If Terrance weren't here, this would be your position."

He slaps me on the back of the helmet as I sprint to the huddle.

Meeting Mike at the left hash, I tell him the play on the way to the huddle on the right hash. I will have the entire wide side of the field to work with. When we get to the huddle, everyone looks freaked out and panicked. Mike shouts, *"Hey, we are not a team made up of one man. Quit looking like a bunch of lost babies. Are we just gonna lie down 'cause Terrance got hurt? We gotta suck it up."*

Everyone in the huddle stands straighter. Mike looks each man in the eye. "Listen, we're running I left 39 pitch. Tommy, get out on that sweep with Sammy and plant that outside linebacker on his ass. Morris here says he'll do the rest." He shoots a smile in my direction. I nod. "All right, here we go. I left 39 pitch on two. I left 39 pitch on two."

We break the huddle and hustle to the line of scrimmage. It's first and ten from the fifteen-yard line. Mike calls the signals: "Red 44. Red 44. Set, hut, hut." When the ball is snapped, I see the inside linebacker inching up for a blitz. Tommy must see it, too, because he decides not to pull and picks him up. That puts Sammy on their outside backer. I move in unison with Sammy Jones and catch the pitch in perfect stride. It's been a while since I played tailback, and I'm used to following Jack, but my instincts take over. Sammy dives at the knees of the outside linebacker and chop blocks him, which puts me one-on-one with their inside backer. Lowering my shoulder, I spin off the hit, a drill I have practiced over and over. The linebacker can't get a hold on me, and I pull loose. Sprinting toward the end zone, the safety takes an angle toward me. The collision will take place around the one-yard line. I lower my shoulder as though I'm going to run over the safety, but at the last second, I jump as high as I can. The safety goes low to meet me and realizes too late that I'm airborne. He stands up at the last second. I am five feet in the air. He catches my left foot, and I spin around like a helicopter in the air. The crowd goes silent, probably unaware that for the moment, they have stopped breathing. I land, safely, in the end zone. Touchdown! The crowd goes wild, hugging each other and giving high fives. The offensive linemen slap my helmet as they congratulate me, relieved, reassured. Our confidence is back.

After that play, the momentum is all ours. Terrance still doesn't feel right and has some trouble standing up. I feel bad for him, but I'm completely jacked up. I want to run the ball again and again. All I can think about is Jack punishing defenders, and on this day, I don't want to be Walter Payton or Jim Brown. I want to be Jack Thompson.

Coach Carlson probably sees the fire in my eyes, and, because of the bad weather, he has no problem giving me the ball. Play after play, I run the ball on counters, sweeps, dives, and traps. Terrance sits out the rest of the game, and I'm in a zone like never before, anticipating blocks and the moves of the defenders. Touching the chain on my neck, under my shoulder pads, I absorb the strength from St. Michael. Like a dragon slayer, on every play I drag two, sometimes three defenders. I tell myself that no one is going to take down this Unionville kid.

By the end of the game, Wooster wants nothing to do with Bertram Academy. I score two more touchdowns, and Mike Giffin throws for another. Wooster scores a touchdown late in the fourth quarter but is never really in the game. We win easily, 28–7.

Coach Carlson huddles us up in the Fawcett Stadium locker room and looks over the team. "Men, we learned a lesson about overcoming adversity today." He pauses. "One of our best players went down, and we rose to the challenge. That's what I love about football. It's a lot like life. You will face a lot of adversity in your life, and you're always going to have a choice about how to react. Do you lie down and feel sorry for yourself? Or do you look inside yourself and say, 'Ain't nothin' goin' to beat me today'?" Coach Kaplan tosses the game ball to Coach Carlson. "Today, a young sophomore rose to that challenge. He stepped up. Game ball goes to Billy Morris. Nice job, son."

My teammates are all looking at me. The crowd noise outside is a muffled hum. But inside that locker room, it's different. It's safe, pure, complete. I miss Unionville, but I've paved a new road for myself at Bertram. I have found a place beyond just being a part of the team, and I have played a respected role, a role that I earned from a summer of hard work and fine-tuning my strengths as a football player.

When we get back to school, it's late. I call Jack's cell phone, but he doesn't answer. I'll have to wait for tomorrow's paper to see whether Unionville won its semifinal game. I have a restless night, anticipating the possibility of playing Unionville in the state championship game.

CHAPTER 29

November 14: Unionville's
Semifinal Playoff Game vs. New Albany

Jack Thompson is playing in the fourth quarter of the state semifinal football game against New Albany at Welcome Stadium in Dayton, Ohio. Unionville is down 7–14 with less than one minute to go in the game. The snow comes down steadily, covering the entire field. Jack gets the ball on a running play to the wide side. His gold number 44 spreads across the front of his royal blue uniform. A torn Kid Rock T-shirt hangs out from under his jersey.

His cleats grab the thin Astroturf as he reads his blocks, eyes widening as he sees a path to the end zone, breathing hard as he turns the corner, squaring his shoulders when he turns up field. He's hoping that someone will come up and hit him, challenge him, so he can lower his shoulder and hurt him, punish him, knock him senseless, make him feel the pain that he feels.

The fans cheer and scream. The stands are loaded with moms, dads, sisters, brothers, the marching band, and just about the entire town of Unionville. The blue and gold colors cover the stands. One crazed parent has an air horn that screeches above the noise. The kids shake milk jugs filled with pennies and scream at the top of their lungs.

Jack bursts through the defense and rumbles into the end zone for a touchdown that makes the score: Unionville 13 New Albany 14. After he scores, Unionville decides to go for a two-point conversion and the win. Despite the insanity of the crowd, inside the huddle, it is quiet, an atmosphere created by trust, discipline, hard work, and love.

In the huddle, the players hold hands. Everybody watches the quarterback, Danny Towers. His eyes scan the team as he says, "Listen, fellas. Let's do this! Punch it in! One time!" He calls the play: "Pro right 38 sweep on two. Pro right 38 sweep on two." It's the same play they just ran. The defense knows Jack is getting the ball, and they know that they can do nothing to stop him. The offense claps their hands, one time, in unison. They sprint to the line of scrimmage, eyes blazing. They have worked too hard for this opportunity. They taste victory, and they want Jack to be the hero. Danny calls the signals: "Red 88. Red 88. Set, hut, hut."

The ball is snapped. The offensive linemen explode from their stances and fire off the line. They grunt from their hearts, their souls, destroying the team across from them as Danny pitches the ball to Jack. He is one on one with their free safety. The safety knows that it's his job to come up and make the hit, but he sees who has the ball and only pretends to give chase. He wants nothing to do with the force of energy that Jack Thompson has become. Jack lumbers into the end zone for the win, 15–14.

Unionville heads to the locker room with helmets raised in celebration. In the locker room, Coach Murphy, cheeks filled with chewing tobacco, unshaven, loved by everyone, addresses the team. "Way to go! You boys did something tonight that has never been done before in the history of our school. You'll be playing for a state championship. You know, it's amazing what you can do when you don't care who gets the credit, when you play for your teammates and not just yourself. Don't ever forget that. Keep it locked in your minds, in your hearts." He pauses to catch his breath. He adjusts his hat, takes it all in. "I want each and every one of you to know that I love you guys. You've made this season an amazing experience for the coaches, and for the entire town. These are memories you will never forget."

The linebacker coach, Coach Miller, tosses Coach Murphy a football. Coach Murphy looks over the entire team and says, "Time for the game ball."

Each player suggests someone else for the recognition. They are the definition of a team. He tosses the ball, referee style, to Jack. "Thompson. Heck of a game, son."

Jack lowers his head. Danny Towers, Woody Fletcher, and Tombo Howard pound on his shoulder pads. Jack doesn't even smile.

On the way to the bus with Tombo and Woody, Jack sees his dad, leaning up against his '57 Chevy, a car his dad rebuilt with his own hands, from the wheels to the engine to the metallic black paint job. Mr. Thompson has been drinking whiskey from the flask that bulges from the inside pocket of his denim jacket. "Did you see my boy?" he brags loudly to anyone who will listen. "He was kickin' some ass tonight. Not as tough as his old man, but it'll do."

Jack tries to look away from his father before their eyes meet.

"Come over here, boy. What? You embarrassed to be seen with your dad? You too good for your old man? Big football star?" His husky voice stops Jack, unlike any player on the field can.

Parents avoid the scene as they head to their cars. Mr. Thompson walks over to his son and leans into him, putting his arm around him, breathing his whiskey breath into his son's face.

"Come on. I'll give you a ride home. Just put the finishing touches on the Chevy. She's running like a top."

Coach Murphy approaches from the side of the bus. "Mr. Thompson," he begins, "team policy is that all athletes ride home on the bus."

Mr. Thompson slurs, "Who do you think you are?"

Coach Murphy, the six foot four inch, ex-Division I football player, looks down at Mr. Thompson and says, "The coach, looking out for my players."

"Yeah, well, I'm his father."

Coach Murphy is close enough that he can smell Mr. Thompson's breath. "Why don't you get a ride home with one of the other parents? I'm sure someone would be happy to drive you home." Coach Murphy goes off to find a parent to take Mr. Thompson home.

"Dad, get a ride with the Howards. They'll take you home," Jack says.

"I ain't no charity case," says Mr. Thompson, as he walks toward his car with his keys in hand.

"Dad, don't drive home," Jack says, pleading with his father.

Mr. Thompson waves off his son as he slides into his '57 Chevy and starts it up. He revs the engine. It purrs and roars at the same time. Giant snowflakes continue to fall and cover the ground. Mr. Thompson peels out; the back end of his car fishtails, just missing a parked minivan near the exit of the parking lot.

Coach Murphy returns with a parent who is willing to take Mr. Thompson home, but he realizes he's too late. He shakes his head, looks over at Jack, and says, "He'll be all right."

Jack throws his bag on the equipment van and climbs onto the team bus.

Mr. Thompson drives east on Route 35 toward 42 North. He squeezes the hard leather ball on the gearshift and pushes on the accelerator, proving to himself that he has built a good car, that he can do something right. The car smoothly switches gears like the well-crafted machine that it is. He smiles, reminds himself that he is a master technician. He curses all the managers who didn't hire him to work at their shops. Morons, he thinks to himself.

His mind drifts to the game and to his son, who is so much his opposite. His son is a great athlete: strong, gifted, talented, and well liked. He loves his son, but at the same time he resents him, because his son has become everything he never was. He believes he has failed as a father and a husband. He pounds on his son and tells him he's a *loser. Damn it, he wants to feel in control of something. He pushes his foot harder on the accelerator and watches the speed climb to eighty miles per hour. He thinks about his wife and the night she left him, how he blamed Jack, knowing it was not his son's fault.*

He pushes down harder on the accelerator, flying by the few cars on Route 35 that have braved the snow-covered roads. The speedometer climbs to ninety. He knows he's in danger, but he doesn't care. He's numb. His chest is tight, and he considers whether he even has a heart. He thinks to himself, what keeps this bag of bones alive?

That question runs through his mind just before his car hits a patch of ice. The front left wheel is the first to lose control. His reaction is slow, almost as if he doesn't want to react. He presses on the brakes, but he's going too fast. His body stiffens, knowing that his speed and the ice are a terrible combination. The car begins to spin in circles on the freeway. Mr. Thompson sees a giant light pole out of the corner of his eye. There is a shattering of glass, a loud pop, and the crunching of metal.

The school bus takes a different route back to Unionville, because the bus driver hears on the radio that a bad accident is blocking Route 35. Jack eases back into his seat, wondering why the bus is taking a different path back to school. He looks out the window of the bus and thinks about playing in the state championship. He thinks about his dad, hoping that things will get better for him. He knows he's a good man. He's seen the good side of him when he isn't drinking. But the alcohol has a hold on him.

Jack wants his mom to come home. He wants things to be "normal." That word spins in his mind … "normal." The bus crawls along the slippery road, making its way back to Unionville.

CHAPTER 30

November 15

My alarm clock wakes me at 7:00 a.m. I jump out of bed and make my routine Saturday trip to the library. On my way, I see a message on my phone from Jack and a text message that reads: Call Me. Before I check the voicemail, I notice that Taylor is waiting for me, only she's not her usual smiling self. She's crying, and her head is buried in her hands. She gives me the paper, but it's not the sports section. It's the front page, which reads: Unionville's Thompson Dies in Car Accident. For a moment, I can't catch my breath. My eyes scan the article:

THE DAYTON FLYER

After Unionville's big win on Friday night, all the celebrating came to an abrupt end with the news of a deadly car accident. Jim Thompson, father of standout football player Jack Thompson, was pronounced dead at Miami Valley Hospital at 11:15 p.m. Last night, weather conditions were poor and visibility was low. Jim Thompson's car slid off Route 35 and hit a light pole on a stretch of freeway just outside Xenia. Severe head injuries, reports say, indicate that death was probably instant. Jim Thompson leaves behind his wife and son.

I try to hold back the tears but can't. A hole has been seared into my stomach. Taylor hugs me and says, "I am so sorry."

I sit there for what seems like an eternity, not wanting to leave Taylor's arms, yet I want to run away.

"I need some air," I tell her, and I walk out onto the campus like a zombie. Pulling the collar of my coat around my neck, I walk into the winter cold, trying to figure out what to say to Jack. What can I say? I walk for an hour. The wind is blowing, and the snow is deep. I don't know what to do.

I go to my dorm. Kevin is not there, so I figure now is as good a time as any. I call Jack, and the phone rings about four or five times until his subdued voice answers, "Billy."

"I read the paper. I can't believe it."

Jack is quiet. Then he says, "My old man grabbed me by the jacket and asked me if I wanted to ride with him. I could smell the liquor on his breath. He had his silver flask hanging out of his pocket. I was so pissed off at him. I didn't know what to do. Coach Murphy stepped in and said team policy is that I ride home on the bus. He could tell that my old man was drinking. He asked my dad to get a ride home with one of the other parents, but my old man would have nothing to do with it. He said he was fine, that he felt great, didn't need anybody's charity. He said nothing could bother him after his son got Unionville to the state championship. Parents offered to drive him home. He shouted that he was fine, and he peeled out of the stadium parking lot. I got the news last night when a policeman told me my dad was dead."

"I'm sorry, man. Are you doing okay?"

"I don't know. There's a picture of the car in the newspaper today. The thing is crunched up like an accordion. The front of the car is pushed up to the steering wheel. It seems like a bad dream. I keep thinking if I go back to sleep, I'll wake up from the nightmare. The only problem is, I can't sleep."

"Just keep breathing."

"It was bound to happen. He was driving on a suspended license. He shouldn't have been driving."

"What are you going to do?"

"Well, a bunch of the guys from the team just left. Now it's just me and Tombo, sitting on the couch, watching the clock, trying to understand all this," Jack says.

I think about *A Prayer for Owen Meany* and the questions Mr. Tanner has asked: What does one believe when faith and doubt come into conflict? Is there a God? And how could God do something like this? I say, "You're going to be all right."

Through the phone, I hear a noise in the background at Jack's house.

Jack says, "Hold on one second. Somebody's at the door."

The line is quiet, and then I hear a woman's voice say, "Are you okay?"

I hold my breath and wait.

Jack gets back on the phone. "Billy, can I call you back? My mom's here."

"Man, that's great news," I say. "Call me later."

"Later."

Jack hangs up. I hit the "End" button on my cell phone and look up at my dorm-room ceiling. I exhale deeply and feel a sense of relief. Jack's mom is home. I figure maybe there is a God, and he comes through in times of need.

I sit on the edge of my bed and rub my eyes. There are so many questions. Why did this happen? Is Jack going to be okay? How will Jack and his mom get through this? Will Jack even consider playing in the state championship game on Friday?

That night, my phone rings. It's Jack, sounding better than when I talked to him earlier.

"Hey, man," I answer.

"Billy, my mom's coming home."

"That's awesome."

It seems like Jack wants to tell me everything at once. "She says she never really left. She was always close by but didn't know how to deal with my dad. She keeps apologizing."

"What are you guys going to do?" I ask.

"She has an apartment near downtown Dayton. We'll probably stay there for a while. I need to get out of this house. It's tough being here." The phone goes silent for a few seconds. Then Jack says, "You know, I loved my dad. He just didn't know how to make things right. If you really knew him, he was a good guy. I'll never forget the look in his eyes after that last playoff game. I could tell how proud he was of me. He stood up straighter, walked taller."

I remain silent.

"He loved coming to those games. For the last couple of months, it seemed like that was what he lived for. You know, one day, he even told me he wanted to get sober, make things right in his life, but he wanted to wait. He said that if he checked into the rehab clinic, he would have to stay there for thirty days, and he didn't want to miss any of my games. He said he didn't want to be in some AA meeting while his boy was winning the biggest game of his life. He didn't want to miss any of it."

Because I feel like I have learned a lot about dealing with situations that are out of my control, I tell him, "There's nothing you can do to bring your dad back. All you can do is live the best way you know how. Don't make the same mistakes he made. Make him proud. Be the man that he would have wanted you to be. That's the best gift you can give your dad."

"My mom is back, and I want to try to help make things right."

"So the plan is to move into her apartment, start over?"

"Yeah, I guess so." It's then that Jack brings up what I hesitated to address earlier: the state championship football game. Considering everything that's happened, it seems so unimportant. "Hey, can you believe it's going to happen? Can you believe we play you guys in the state championship game on Friday night?"

"I know. It's crazy. Never in a million years could I ever have imagined it. When I left three months ago, I wanted nothing more than to play for Unionville, and now here I am, playing against you guys."

"It will be like the first day of hitting during double sessions, me versus you."

"It'll be a battle, for sure."

"I can't wait."

"Are you actually considering playing?"

"Who me?" Jack asks.

"Yeah, you."

"Are you kidding?" he says. "That game ... that game ... I wouldn't miss that game for anything in the world. With everything that's happened with my dad, it's the *one* thing keeping me alive."

CHAPTER 31

November 17: The Funeral

Outside, the wind blows hard, and the snow falls heavy on the little white church in the middle of Unionville. The temperature outside is about thirty degrees. Inside the church, it doesn't feel much warmer.

Jack Thompson sits on the cold, hard bench in the first row of the church. His father's casket sits about five feet to his right, with an American flag draped over it. Jack holds his mother's hand, and she gives his hand a strong squeeze. The church is filled with coaches and players from the football team. Tombo and Woody sit close to Jack. The community has rallied around the football team all season, and now they have come to support Jack. Jack wishes his best friend could be there, but he knows that Billy has no way of getting there from Bertram.

Jack thinks about the other funerals in his family. He barely remembers when his grandma passed away, because he was only four years old at the time. When he was ten years old, his grandpa died. Even though it was only six years ago, it seems like a lifetime away. He doesn't remember much about his grandpa, other than the fact that his grandpa died a drunk. Whenever Jack would go to visit, the television was always on. His grandpa would sit in the *shadows, as though he were allergic to the light. Grandpa Joe would never go outside, and he spent the last year of his life in bed, with a bottle of whiskey always close by. Jack could never understand that existence. But then Jack saw his father become a younger version of his grandpa. Younger and stronger of course, but he still had the same addiction: the pull of the alcohol, the power of the drink.*

The priest stands at the altar and begins the service with a prayer. "Lord, we are gathered here today to remember the life of Jim Thompson."

While the priest's words blend together, Jack thinks back to the days before the death of his father. The DUIs, the late nights at The Tavern, his father's constant arguing with his mother, and the night his father hit his mother, causing her to leave both of them because she didn't know what else to do. He thinks about all the days his father spent hanging around the house and working on that '57 Chevy after being fired from his last job. Living with his father was never easy, but as Jack got older, it became more and more difficult. It was when his father finally lost his job at the garage that he dropped off quickly. The six-pack became the whiskey, and the verbal insults became the physical abuse.

Jack can't help but remember the night his father died. In his mind, he can see the snow coming down in the parking lot just outside the stadium. He can see the smile on his father's face after the game, knowing his son's performance was the reason Unionville would be playing for a state championship. Jack could have been in that car, and then he would be in a casket right next to his father. It was

Coach Murphy who said that all players must ride home on the team bus. Team policy. That was it. The defining moment.

Jack's thoughts are interrupted when an older woman with curly gray hair begins playing a song on the organ, one that Jack does not recognize. Each note is long and drawn out, filling the tiny church. The song seems to fit the mood: dark, sad, and full of regret.

A tear slides down his mother's cheek, and Jack wonders how she can feel anything but anger toward the man who was a constant source of first verbal and then physical abuse. Holding her hand, Jack can feel his mother's body shake.

Jack can feel his own anxiety, as he turns into himself, away from the outside world.

The priest delivers the sermon and attempts to make a tribute to the life of Mr. Thompson.

Jack can only consider that his father didn't do much right. What in his father's life was there to celebrate?

But the priest begins to talk about his father's selfless service to his country. When the priest talks about his father's military service, Jack sees a different side of his father. He understands that his father was young once, fearless, willing to defend his country at any price. And for a moment, Jack does feel a sense of pride. He looks at the flag that drapes over the casket, and the red stripes and stars seem brighter. Even though his dad did a lot of things wrong, Jack knows that his father did some things right, and that gives him a sense of peace.

When the sermon is over, the gray-haired lady plays "Amazing Grace." Jack contemplates the lyrics of the song and thinks about his life. How he's been living. His drinking. His disregard for Leigh. This insight is Jack's vision ... about how he's living ... his new direction in life. Deep down, Jack knows that something inside him has to change. He just doesn't know how to go about making those changes. Looking long and hard at the casket, he knows that unless he changes, his life won't be any different from his father's.

When the service is over, Jack and his mother follow the men pushing the casket to the front door of the church, followed by members of the football team and the rest of the community, where he and some men from the funeral home guide the casket into the back of the hearse.

At the cemetery, Jack, Tombo, Woody and three other men from the funeral home, lift the casket from the back of the hearse. The weight of the casket is heavy in Jack's hand. It's more than just the weight of the casket and the body—it's the weight of an early death. But Jack knows, somehow, that being there and doing this for his father is important. Jack, Woody, Tombo, and the other men set the casket down on top of the wide green bands that stretch over the top of the grave.

The priest says a short prayer and then sprinkles some dirt on top of the casket. Each person in attendance places a single flower on the casket, and then, quietly, they make their way back to their cars.

On the ride home from the funeral, Jack sits next to his mom. She wears a pair of oversized sunglasses, but Jack can see the streaks on her face from the tears.

"Are you okay?" Jack asks.

His mom takes a tissue and dabs at the mascara on her cheeks. "I'm fine," she says, letting out a deep breath.

"Why are you so upset?" Jack asks. "I thought you hated Dad."

"We were together for a long time. You don't just stop loving someone." Jack's mom nods her head, as if she's agreeing with her own statement. "He was different when we first met. So full of life."

"So you still loved him?"

"Not like I used to. At one time, he was my best friend. I'm not ashamed of that." His mom pauses and pats her son on the knee. "Do me a favor," she says.

"Sure, anything, Mom. You know that."

"Don't make the same mistakes he made."

Jack sits back in his seat, wondering how to avoid that fate. His dad's behavior is what he knows, but he knows one other thing: he doesn't want to end up like his dad, alone and dead.

As Jack and his mom drive down the road to her apartment, Jack thinks about the fact that most of the people who attended his father's funeral were Jack's friends. He thinks about how sad it is that his dad did not have many friends of his own.

And then an idea pops into Jack's head. Maybe there is a way that he can start over. Maybe he can change everything about his life, including where he lives. He thinks about his best friend, Billy Morris, and wonders whether Bertram Academy would ever take a kid like Jack Thompson.

CHAPTER 32

November 17ᵗʰ

Mr. Tanner looks at me as I walk into class. I can't get the thought of the death of Jack's father out of my mind. I wish that things were as they were before. I wish that things could be right for Jack.

"Good morning," he says. "Come on in. Have a seat. I hope everyone had a good weekend. I know the football team must be excited for the state championship football game on Friday night." There is a rumble of discussion around the room. "We have two more chapters of *A Prayer for Owen Meany*. I trust all of you have done the reading, and most of you are engaged by—if nothing else—the voice of Owen." The class laughs at the high-pitched voice of Owen and how, for his small size, he is able to have such a huge impact on everyone in his life.

From the back of the room, Amanda, a field hockey player, says, "It's one of those books that you wish never ended." The class chuckles, but no one disagrees. I think everyone identifies with the book. It is hard to ignore the voice of Owen and his dilemma. He is a self-proclaimed instrument of God.

After thinking about Owen, I contemplate the role of God in my life, the role of fate, and the roles of other people in my life. I think about my mom and how her life was so changed by Richard and how that brought me here to Bertram. I think about Cindy and what I thought love was, and then I think about Taylor. She has become so much a part of my life in such a short time. As I look over at her on the other side of the room, even early on Monday morning, she is amazing. But on my mind more than anything is the death of Jack's father.

I stop to talk to Mr. Tanner after class.

"Mr. Morris, what's on your mind?"

"Too much."

He tilts his head to look me in the eye. "What's up?"

"It's just," I pause, "my best friend back home. His dad died this weekend."

Mr. Tanner doesn't seem affected by this news. I guess after two tours in Vietnam, nothing really shocks you. "What happened?" he asks.

"He died on Friday night in a drunk-driving accident."

"I'm sorry. I didn't know." Mr. Tanner drops his head and then looks up at me sympathetically. "I have to tell you something," he says, his face getting serious. "When I was in the war, I saw some senseless death. I saw some really bad things, things that still keep me up at night, more than thirty years later. Sometimes people die, and there isn't a thing we can do about it. Sometimes the Lord takes over, and we just have to accept the results. I'm not saying it's right or fair. That's just the way it is."

"I'm just worried about my friend. I don't know how he's going to deal with it."

"Let me tell you a story," he begins. "My best friend and I, we didn't get drafted into Vietnam—we volunteered. We thought we were tough, bad asses, you know. Well nothing, and I mean nothing, can prepare someone for the things that went on in Vietnam. So we end up in the same platoon, best friends full of energy, fearless, going to bust some Communist ass. We think we're so tough. We strut around the base like we aren't afraid of anything. So we're in-country for only two weeks, and we get into this ground attack. Bullets are flying, and I'm ducking for cover. In the middle of the ambush, I look over and see my best friend, Joey Porter, all shot up, laying there with a hole the size of a coconut in his gut. All of a sudden, I'm not so tough anymore. In fact, I'm scared, more afraid than I've been in my life. I want to be home right then. There I am, nineteen years old, feeling completely paralyzed."

"What did you do?"

"I just kept praying, praying to just keep breathing. Get Joey out of there; get myself home in one piece. That's why I'm so into religion. When I started praying on the field in Khe Sanh, something happened to me. An energy, a force came to me. It wrapped itself around me, and it told me that everything was going to be okay. When I finished my tour, I became very religious. It wasn't any one religion in particular, just a belief in a higher power. I combined everything to form my own belief system. But something saved me, something that wasn't of this world, something that transcended anything that I had ever known. And that, I have to believe in."

I think I understand what Mr. Tanner is saying. He wants me to have faith, to believe in a higher power, and to use my meditation. But more importantly, I have to realize that the healing and strength are going to come from inside me, from within my own heart. I have to be willing to do the same thing for Jack. I have to help him realize that despite all the things that have happened to him, he's going to be okay. There's no reason he can't get through this. After all, when all is said and done, what do we have to fall back on? Our faith. I'm not exactly sure what that means for me, but I get the feeling that this experience is going to help me figure all that out.

Mr. Tanner stands up and puts his hand on my shoulder. He looks me directly in the eyes and says, "You and your buddy are going to be all right."

I nod my head.

"If you need anything, you know where you can find me."

I thank him and head to the hallway. Taylor is standing there waiting. She walks up to me, and without saying anything, she hugs me.

We walk to our next class through the early-morning cold. The snow blankets the ground, and the wind whips through the center of campus.

"Are you doing okay?" she asks.

"I'll be fine. I'm worried about Jack."

"He's going to be okay. Just be a good friend, and be there for him as much as you can."

"I wish I could have been there for him at the funeral."

"You had no way of getting there. There was only so much you could do." Taylor puts her arm around me. "I'm really sorry all this has happened. Know that I'm here for you."

"Thanks."

"No problem," she says, trying to lighten the mood.

Her simple gesture makes me feel better.

We get to the music and art building and head to our separate classes. "I'll talk to you later," I say.

"Let me know if you need anything."

My week begins, and the days are filled with classes and tests, until Thursday, when the school has a huge pep rally. Students and teachers cheer as each player is introduced. The small pep band plays a fight song, and the headmaster addresses the school.

He talks about what a great journey the football team has taken the school on and how the team has brought an energy and excitement to the entire Bertram community. But during his speech and in the middle of all that excitement, my mind drifts to Jack and playing against him in the biggest game of my life.

CHAPTER 33
November 21

The day of the Division II Ohio State Championship arrives. We load the bus and begin the two-and-a-half hour bus ride to The Ohio State University in Columbus. Terrance Strong, Sammy Jones, and Marcus Tyler sit stone-faced in the back of the bus with their headphones on. This is their second time playing in a state championship game. The bus is quiet as we drive through Canton and pass the Pro Football Hall of Fame. The snow falls lightly, dusting the interstate on our way to Columbus.

On the ride down, I think about Jack and playing against my best friend in what will be the biggest football game of our lives. I reflect on the insane journey that started that day in my kitchen. I can still hear my mother's words: *"Billy, come in the kitchen. There's something we need to talk about."* I can still remember Richard standing behind my mother as she calmly explained that we would be leaving Unionville. My chest tightens, and my heart sinks while I ride on the Bertram bus almost four months later.

On the ride to Columbus, I think about meeting Kevin and Taylor, and what a difference they have made in my life. I reflect on my now famous battle with Terrance Strong. I think about Mr. Tanner and the hours I've spent meditating, how the meditation and how the books we've read in class have helped to transform my life. I think about Jack's father, his pushing Jack around and telling him that he was nothing. I remember Jack's baseball game, when the police escorted Mr. Thompson from the game in their cruiser, and how at the end of the game, on the way back to the school, Jack said, "Sometimes... I wish he were dead." Sometimes, you have to be careful about what you wish for. You might just get it.

The bus rolls onto the Ohio State campus and down Olentangy Boulevard, making its way through the city on its way to the stadium. The bus driver pulls into the parking lot that surrounds the Horseshoe, the stadium of The Ohio State Buckeyes. We file off the bus, and the team managers bring out a bag of footballs. We get the lay of the land, jogging around the field as a team with just our warm-ups on. The wind whistles through the end of the stadium, and light rain falls on and off. I partner up with Kevin and do some stretching.

After throwing the ball and running around the field, Coach Carlson shouts, "Let's bring it in." We huddle up around him at the fifty-yard line on top of the giant O. "Men, look around you. Take it all in, the opportunity of a lifetime." He pauses, looks around the giant stadium, and breathes in the cold winter air. "We're going to the hotel to check in. We'll be there for about four hours, and then we'll come back."

As I exit the stadium, I take a second to look around at more than one hundred thousand empty seats, imagining what it would be like to play for the Buckeyes in front of a packed crowd on a Saturday night. My version of that game is just seven hours away. A steady flurry of snow begins to cover the artificial turf, mixing with the rain. Like Coach Carlson, I take a deep breath and savor the moment, and exhale, watching my breath float up into the sky.

Before I get on the bus, I see a yellow school bus pull into the far end of the parking lot. It's the Unionville bus. A huge lump sits in my throat. Images of Jack, Woody, Tombo, Coach Murphy, and Coach Miller flash through my head.

The bus stops at the opposite entrance, and the Unionville team, led by Coach Murphy, exits the bus. The blue and gold letter jackets file off one by one. I squint to get a glimpse of my buddies, until I hear the voice of Coach Carlson. "Morris, let's go."

I turn away and step up on the stairs of the bus, take one last look, and head back to my seat.

Back at the hotel, Kevin and I share a room. We throw our bags down and sit on our separate double beds. "How are things going?" I ask.

"Okay, I guess," Kevin says.

"You ready to play?"

"Yeah, man. This is what it's about." The tone of his voice suggests a completely different answer.

"Dude, I'm nervous as hell. I can't believe we're playing Unionville."

"I can't imagine what it would be like playing against my best friends. How are you holding up?"

"Man, playing in The Shoe at Ohio State, it's like a dream come true. I just never thought it would be against my old team. Part of me wants to be playing with those guys. Part of me wants to take the field wearing the blue and gold. Ever since I was little, I've wanted to play in a state championship for Unionville. Unionville's in my blood."

Kevin nods his head. "I can see wanting to play with your buddies. I don't blame you."

"You know, everyone at Bertram is so serious. They forget what it's all about— having fun. Jack and those guys work hard and all, but when it comes time to play, they have a blast. They just let it rip. They get fired up. I miss that."

"Yeah, but these guys at Bertram know what it takes. They've been here before."

"I guess you're right, but shouldn't it be fun, too?" I ask.

"I wouldn't worry about it." Kevin grabs the remote from the table between the two beds and turns on the television to watch ESPN.

I stare at the ceiling and think about the game. Unlike Kevin, I am worried.

Five o'clock arrives, and we grab our stuff.

We load up the bus as the sun is setting, but by the time we get to the stadium, I notice the blue-black clouds hovering over the Ohio State campus and the snow turning to a freezing rain. We circle the parking lot and stop by the locker room entrance.

Coach Carlson stands up. He wears a large, red coat with a silver eagle on the back. He holds his clipboard in his hand and says, "Men, let's head to the locker room and get suited up, and then we'll go through our warm-up."

We walk into the visiting team's locker room. It isn't anything special: big lockers, showers, and chalkboards with Xs and Os all over the place, urgent markings from the Division IV game that was played before ours.

After I get dressed and tape my wrists, Coach Kaplan huddles the defense together and goes over the Unionville offense. Coach Carlson gathers the offense together and goes over how to attack Unionville's defense.

Coach Carlson speaks to the entire team before we take the field. "Men—and I do mean men—I have seen this team become more than just good football players. This team has become a group of hard-working, dedicated young men. You guys have applied yourselves like no team I have ever coached. You should all be proud of that. Tonight … tonight, let's put it together. Let's win another state championship. Let's make all the folks back at Bertram proud. Make your parents proud. More importantly, make yourself proud. Make this night extraordinary. Make it a night you'll never forget. Seniors, this is your time. Be the leaders you know you can be. Let's go! Bring it in!"

The team comes together in the middle of the locker room, and we say the Lord's Prayer. Then we huddle up, and we all put our hands in. The seniors shout, "Let's go! Get it up!" Everyone yells and shouts, but I can't help but notice that something is missing.

We fill the tunnel on the opposite side of the stadium from Unionville. I look out onto the lit-up field. As we jog onto the field, I can tell that the rain and freezing temperatures have made the turf slippery, a disadvantage for our outside running game. Our disadvantage will be Unionville's advantage. Because the conditions will benefit Jack and his downhill running style, we are in for one hell of a game.

I glance around the stadium. The fans pack the first two sections of seating all the way around the stadium. There are probably close to twenty thousand people. I have never played in front of this many people in my life. The Bertram fans are going crazy. Red and gray colors decorate the stands. The Unionville fans match their intensity. Royal blue and gold colors are scattered throughout their seats. I catch a glimpse of Cindy. She's wearing a varsity letter jacket over her cheerleading outfit. I notice my mom sitting in the Bertram stands with Jack's mother. I look around, but I don't see Richard. With so much going on, it's almost impossible to focus on the game.

I catch punts at the fifty-yard line, until I see Jack coming toward me. I jog over to him, and without uttering a word, we hug each other. It's good to see my best friend.

"So this is it?" Jack says.

"Yeah, this is what we worked for. I never thought things would play out like this."

Jack drops his head. "Yeah, well, not much makes sense to me lately."

"You can say that again. I'm sorry about your dad."

Jack looks me in the eye. "Yeah, me, too." Jack adjusts his black wristbands over his forearms. "Hey, I gotta get back to the team. Good luck, man."

"Yeah, you, too."

He jogs over to his offensive huddle, where Coach Murphy sends in plays for the pregame warm-up.

As I jog over to our defensive huddle, Coach Kaplan blows his whistle. The scout offense runs some of Unionville's plays, which I know by heart. I stand in the back of the huddle and hear someone yelling my name.

"Go get 'em, Billy. Go get 'em!"

It's Taylor. She waves from the stands, sitting with her friends from the field hockey team. I have to pinch myself to make sure I'm not dreaming: Taylor, the state championship football game, my best friend, and the opportunity of a lifetime.

After our fifteen-minute warm-up, the captains take the field for the coin toss. Unionville wins the toss and chooses to receive. We will be on defense first. Coach

Carlson brings us together on the sideline. "Come on, men. Let's make it happen. Let's make it happen."

Filled with adrenaline and anticipation, we sprint out to our kickoff positions. We kick the ball deep, and Johnny Phillips runs it to the thirty-yard line before Kevin brings him down with a solid hit.

Marcus calls our defensive play: "52 slant, eagle, man. 52 slant, eagle, man."

Unionville breaks out of its huddle and sprints to the line of scrimmage. The massive bodies line up against each other. My heart pounds as if it wants to burst from my chest. The linemen get into their three-point stances. Jack lines up deep in the backfield, the position that I had earned earlier this summer. I look into his eyes, but they are not his. He has made some kind of sick transformation. On the first play, Jack gets the handoff over the right tackle. He bursts through the line of scrimmage and blasts right through our biggest defensive lineman, a six foot five inch, 295-pound hulk, like he isn't even there. He continues his running assault, carrying two or three defenders for another ten yards. He jumps to his feet unfazed and sprints back to the huddle.

Play after play, they give Jack the ball on dives, sweeps, and off-tackle blasts. With each run, he seems to get stronger, enjoying the physical and violent contact. Jack is fueled by more than the muscles he built up over the season. He is driven by the death of his father, and he has picked this night to unleash everything that has been bottled up inside of him. In many ways, Jack seems larger than life.

His powerful legs break through tackles, and he lowers his shoulder, relentlessly punishing would-be tacklers. The loudspeakers echo throughout the stadium: *"Jack Thompson the ball carrier."* Unionville picks up first down after first down. Over and over, the voice repeats the same words: *"Jack Thompson the ball carrier."* And his running assault continues.

Unionville drives all the way to our two-yard line. There's not much talk between the two teams, but there's a lot of talk within the teams. Unionville's players celebrate with high fives, as we point fingers and blame each other. Even though it's early in the game, we already feel a sense of urgency. We know that we cannot withstand four quarters of Jack Thompson. On first and goal from the two, they run a tailback trap. I read the trap block and shoot into the hole. The play isolates me against Jack. The collision is like an explosion. Jack lowers his shoulder and blasts into me. The pop of the pads travels across the field. He pounds his way through me and over me, stepping into the end zone. I roll over and watch as Jack hands the ball to the referee. Standing up, I try to steady myself with wobbly knees and a dazed expression. The announcer's voice booms through the stadium: *"Touchdown Unionville. Jack Thompson on the carry for the Rockets."*

Unionville kicks the extra point to make the score, 7–0.

Our offense is not as effective as Unionville's punishing ground game. The freezing rain and the cold night-time temperatures create a thin layer of ice on the turf. On our first play, a wide sweep to the right, Terrance's feet come out from under him as he slips on the frozen surface. The cold wind and rain prevent us from throwing effectively, and the icy turf doesn't allow our running backs to make sharp cuts.

After Jack's touchdown, our defense begins to come together, and we start gang-tackling Jack, who drags two, three, sometimes four defenders. The voice over the loudspeaker continues: *"Jack Thompson the ball carrier."*

The second quarter is a back-and-forth exchange of punts and short drives. With only a few seconds left in the half, Coach Murphy goes into his bag of trick plays and calls one that I have never seen before. Unionville runs the hook and ladder with an option thrown into it. These plays usually never work, especially under such horrible conditions. The wide receiver does a twelve-yard hook, while the slotback comes behind him, and the other wide receiver trails behind the slotback for the option. We contain the hook and ladder, but it is the option that breaks the play all the way down to our one-yard line. Terrance runs down a streaking Woody Fletcher and pushes him out of bounds at the one-yard line, but two seconds remain on the clock.

Both teams huddle up. Everyone in the stadium knows who is going to get the ball. Unionville breaks the huddle and sprints to the line of scrimmage. We get set, anticipating Jack getting the ball on a dive or sweep. He only needs one yard for the touchdown.

Danny Towers calls the signals: "Blue 22. Blue 22. Set, hut, hut." He sprints to his left to hand the ball off to Jack. Jack plows over the left side of the line, pushing the heap of bodies. Our defense pushes back with everything we have. When the play finally comes to an end, the announcer's voice thunders over the loudspeakers and echoes throughout the stadium: *The Bertram Eagles stop Jack Thompson on the carry.* The time expires, and somehow, we manage to keep Jack out of the end zone.

We are down 7–0 at the half, but our attitudes tell a different story, something more like 70–0. We enter the locker room with heads down and spirits broken. There's no explosion from Terrance Strong. The silence in the locker room is deafening.

Terrance comes up to me and says, "Morris, it's like a bad dream. And your boy, Thompson, he's killing us."

I don't even respond. Coach Carlson comes into the locker room and gets down to business. "Men," he begins, "get with your position coaches, and let's figure out how to get back in the game. We are only down seven points." He takes a practical, almost scientific approach to the game: execute, outsmart, and outplay your opponent. His philosophy is simple, but tonight, we need something more. We need a major fire lit under us. And who am I to speak up? For the first fifteen minutes during halftime, coaches draw up plays and ask players how they can make adjustments. Everyone is listening, but nobody seems emotionally attached, as though they really want to win.

Before we head out for the second half, Coach Carlson looks around the locker room and looks into the faces of each player on the team. His jaw tightens. *"Everybody stop."* Surprised, we all turn and look. His eyes look wild, and for the first time all year, he goes off. *"What is going on? Do you guys realize that this is the opportunity of a lifetime? Seniors, this is your last high school football game! In the entire state of Ohio, two teams made it here. Two teams. You have worked too hard and invested too much to blow it now. Don't look back on tonight and wish things had turned out differently. You can change them right now. You can change this to the ending that you want. I want to get one thing across to you guys right now and for the rest of your lives: don't live your lives with any regret. Don't live your lives wishing things were different when you have the power to make them different. No regrets!"*

The expressions change on the guys' faces. Terrance, Marcus, and some of the offensive and defensive linemen start yelling and getting each other fired up. The words sink in. Everyone knows that Coach is right.

Coach Carlson must be inspired by his own speech, because he decides to make some changes. For one, he takes out senior fullback Sammy Jones and puts me in. "Morris," he says, "show me what you can do. I know these guys are your old friends, but this isn't personal. Just play the game."

We take the field for the second half with a different attitude. Unionville kicks off to Terrance, and he runs the kickoff to the twenty-five yard line. I join the offensive huddle. The linemen have a different look on their faces after the coaches explain that the second half is going to be straight ahead, smash-mouth football. I will be Terrance's lead blocker, and I'm ready for the challenge. Terrance grabs me in the huddle and says, "Hey, Morris. You're a bad man. Let's see what you got."

Coach Carlson sends in a succession of inside running plays, plays that do not fit the outside running style of Terrance, but play after play, we pick up first downs. On dive plays, Jack takes me head-on more than once. The collisions are violent and nasty, but the offensive line opens holes. We move down the field. But unlike us, Unionville doesn't point any fingers. They regroup after each play and bring it even harder on the next play. On each play, the offensive and defensive lines fire off the ball, crashing violently into each other. The cold temperature makes me feel each collision down to my bones.

On first and goal from the four-yard line, Coach Carlson calls a fullback dive over our right guard. I take the handoff from Mike Giffin and plow over the right side of the line. I dive headfirst from the two-yard line and extend the ball over the goal line. Touchdown!

On the next play, our kicker hooks the ball to the left, missing the extra point. The score is Bertram 6, Unionville 7.

I see that my boys from Unionville aren't sure what hit them. After dominating the entire first half, they suddenly find themselves in a battle. Our newly energized defense shuts down their offense. Jack still runs hard and manages to pick up a few first downs, but he doesn't dominate like he did in the first half.

The momentum has shifted.

Late in the third quarter, Terrance breaks a dive play for a sixty-yard touchdown run to make the score, 12–7. He gets the handoff, and the hole opens up like the parting of the Red Sea. I throw the block on Jack that springs Terrance, knocking him to the ground.

Terrance puts a move on Woody Fletcher that sends Woody airborne, diving to the ground, grabbing at nothing but air. I stand over Jack after my block.

Jack slowly gets up, looks at me with fire in his eyes, and says, "Game over."

I'm not sure what Jack means, but I get the sense that I'm about to find out. On the next play, Jack breaks through the line like a guided missile and blocks the extra point to keep the score: Bertram 12, Unionville 7.

It's then that Coach Murphy decides to put the game in the hands of his best player—Jack Thompson. Jack gets the ball on play after play. The announcer on the loudspeaker revisits his mantra: *"Jack Thompson the ball carrier."* We have pissed off the giant.

Jack powers through our defense, punishing anyone who tries to tackle him. His forearm is cut up, and there is blood on his pants. His eyes narrow. He bounces off tacklers, stumbles, puts his arm down, and, like a good wrestler, steadies himself before continuing his running assault. On every play, he gets stronger and stronger.

With two minutes left in the game, the score remains, 12-7. Unionville has the ball on our thirty-five-yard line. There's no question that Jack is going to get the ball. Play after play, Jack runs over right tackle, then left tackle. His linemen pick him up and slap him on the helmet as the seconds tick off the clock.

With only thirty seconds remaining on the clock, Unionville has the ball, third down at our six-yard line. Danny Towers runs a bootleg to the right after faking an off-tackle play to Jack. Our whole defense goes after the fake, except for me. I remember the play from practices with Unionville and mirror Danny. He breaks the contain of our defensive end. I see his eyes light up as he sees the end zone. He sprints to the corner pylon, but I take a good angle and come out of nowhere, running him down at the three-yard line and preventing the touchdown. The clock runs down to five seconds, and Unionville calls a timeout.

Coach Kaplan jogs from the sideline into our huddle. His voice is hoarse from a full game of yelling instructions from the sidelines. "This is it, fellas. This is the final play. One play for a state championship! One play for a lifetime. Make it count! Watch for the sweep. They've been running Thompson up the middle all day. They might try to go outside. Corners, we gotta turn the play inside. Linebackers, play inside out. Watch the sweep."

The referee blows his whistle and shouts in a raspy voice, "Let's go, coaches, out of the huddle."

Unionville breaks the huddle and sprints to the line of scrimmage.

Marcus shouts out the defense: "52 slant lion, eagle, thunder! 52 slant lion, eagle, thunder!" I twist my cleats into the turf for better traction.

Danny Towers, his breath turning to smoke in the cold air, calls the signals: "Red 38. Red 38. Set, hut, hut." He takes the snap from the center.

I read my guard, who pulls hard to his left. It's a sweep to the wide side of the field, just like Coach Kaplan anticipated. I play it perfectly. My course is downhill toward the line of scrimmage and inside out. Jack takes the pitch deep in the backfield. He follows his blocks. His eyes widen as he sees the hole open up, a lane right into the end zone. But he doesn't see me coming. I ram hard into his side. It's a textbook hit. My facemask is on the ball, and I drive against him. Jack tries to break through the tackle, pumping his legs like pistons.

Terrance comes up for run support and blasts into Jack and me. Following Terrance is Marcus. Three powerful bodies hammer in hard against Jack, but we aren't driving against another player. We are driving against an emotion, a will, and a desire. Jack refuses to go down. He plants hard on his right foot and explodes with his head down, carrying three of us on his shoulders and back, dragging us, grunting, crying, and refusing to give up. He forces the pile of bodies toward the goal line, down to the three, the two, to the one. When the final play comes to an end, with no time on the clock, Jack lies face down on the turf, one yard deep in the end zone. Touchdown.

Unionville wins, 13 to 12. Game over.

After Jack is mobbed by his Unionville teammates, he hands the ball to the referee and jogs over to the sideline in a trance. Our defense is in the end zone, some pounding the turf with their fists, crying.

The next ten minutes are a blur. Both teams wait until Unionville gets the championship trophy and Bertram receives the runner-up trophy. The Unionville team members congratulate each other. We just watch, wishing we were the ones going home with the win.

After the trophy presentation, in the far end zone, Coach Carlson calls the team together. Obviously disappointed, he begins, "Men, I am proud of your effort. After that first half, you could have quit. You could have given up, but this is a good lesson to take with you—never, under any circumstances, give up. I'm impressed with your desire not to quit. You all showed a great deal of character out there today. You should be proud. You left it all on the field. Seniors, this is it for you. You guys made one hell of a run. Be proud. Juniors, sophomores, use this game to burn your fire a little brighter as you work in the off-season."

I look around at Terrance Strong, Mike Giffin, Sammy Jones, and Marcus Tyler. They shed very real tears of lost opportunity. Even though Coach said we left it all on the field, we all know it isn't true. We all know that we didn't play our best game. We failed to make the most of our opportunity. Despite the tears and regret, the team is not overwhelmed by the loss. Maybe we didn't care enough about the game, or maybe we didn't care enough about each other.

I finally understand what Bertram has been missing. It isn't athletic ability or the desire to win, because everyone at Bertram has that. What we are missing that Unionville has is the desire to win for each other. It's amazing how much harder you play when you are playing for your teammates and your brothers. Unionville players genuinely love each other and are willing to do whatever they have to do to win.

The snow begins to fall again as the teams make their way to the locker room. Jack and I look directly at each other as we meet on the track that surrounds the football field. I extend my hand. In my hand is Jack's silver chain with the St. Michael medal with the angel looking over the two children. Placing it in Jack's hand, I say, "You might need this more than I do." I point to St. Michael on the medal. "You see, there he is fighting that dragon. And what about that angel? You think that angel is looking over us?"

Jack looks at the medal in his hand, nods his head, and forces a smile. "This game was for my dad," he says. "You know, he just didn't know how to get out of it. He wanted to. I could see it. He loved my mom and me. I wish I could've helped him."

"You did what you could."

"Yeah, well, none of this makes any sense."

I look over into the stands and see my mom sitting with Jack's mom.

"I wonder where Richard is," I say.

Jack responds, "My mom said things didn't work out. She says your mom might be moving back to Unionville. What do you think about that?"

"I don't know," I say, stunned.

"Maybe you can come back to Unionville and be with the boys? It's been tough with you being gone."

"Believe me," I begin, "it hasn't been easy for me either. Being away from you guys has been brutal. All season long, I wished I was playing with you guys."

Jack says, "Coach Murphy told us that no matter what happened tonight, that we should know that he loves us and this has been one of the most amazing things in his life. I would do anything for him."

"I know what you mean."

"We'd love to have you back."

"Yeah, it would be good to be back, but it looks like everyone has pretty much moved on."

"What do you mean?"

"I see Cindy got herself a new boyfriend," I say.

Jack nods his head. "Yeah, after you broke up with her, she started dating Danny. I don't think she really likes him. He's just someone to hang out with. She misses you. She tells me all the time."

I think about Taylor and wonder what will happen.

Jack says, "It looks like either way, you can't lose. You have a great school at Bertram, and you've got good friends in Unionville."

"I guess it all depends on what my mom decides to do. You know it's funny, I've met some amazing people here." I think about Taylor, Kevin, and Mr. Tanner.

"No kidding?" And then out of nowhere, Jack says, "Well, maybe I could come to Bertram."

I do a double take. "Really?" I ask.

"Maybe." Jack smiles. "Hey, I gotta get back with the team. Call me and let me know what's happening with you and your mom." We give each other a hug.

"Hey, man. Great game."

"Yeah, you, too," says Jack, as he turns with his helmet in hand and jogs back to the Unionville locker room.

I turn and head toward our locker room. Taylor is waiting by the fence that surrounds the track. She is bundled up in her winter hat, scarf, and gloves.

She leans over and gives me a big hug. "Hey, you guys played hard. I've never seen two teams play as hard as you guys played tonight. It was a great game."

"Thanks," I say. What Taylor says is nice, but I know that sometimes playing well isn't enough. I wanted to win that state championship in the worst way. I wanted to say that we were the best team in the state. I shrug my shoulders and see that Taylor understands so much more about things than I do. She understands that football is just a game, and yet, it's not just about the game. It's the willingness to put everything you've got into something. Even though we lost, I know that I'm a better person for having had the experience. During the playoffs, we played against the best athletes in the state. We competed like warriors and proved that we belonged. We could play with anybody. I realize that Unionville was not necessarily the better team. Maybe if we played them on another night, under different circumstances, we might've won the game.

But Unionville brought something to that stadium tonight, and it was in Jack Thompson's heart. It was his fearlessness that said: *Anything you can dish out won't hurt me, because I've been through something no one should have to go through in a lifetime. Keep trying to knock me down, because I'm coming back every play. And I'm coming back harder each time.*

I hug Taylor and thank her for coming to the game. Before I reach the locker room, I see Mr. Tanner. "Mr. Morris, that was one hell of a game. You guys played tough. I'm really proud of you. You've got nothing to be ashamed of. Keep your head up, son."

Mr. Tanner has a look of true pride, and his words mean everything to me.

"Thanks, Mr. Tanner," I say, and extend my hand.

Tanner shakes my hand and pats me on the back. "I'll catch up with you back at school," he says, as he slips back into the crowd.

I glance over and see my mother approaching me with tears in her eyes. She doesn't even let me speak. "I am so sorry," she begins. "I thought what I was doing was best for everyone. Sometimes, people make mistakes. I wish I could take it all back."

"Mom, I understand."

My mother stops me again. "I want to make things right. I want to make things good again."

"Where do we go from here?" I ask.

"Well, Jack's mom and I talked about Jack finishing this semester at Unionville, and then maybe him going to Bertram."

I think to myself, the best of both worlds: a great school with Jack and Taylor.

"So what happened to Richard?" I ask.

"We didn't see eye to eye on a lot of things."

Nodding my head, I say, "I'll talk to you when I get back to school."

My mom heads toward the parking lot, and I start walking toward the locker room. Most of the fans have cleared out of the stadium. Some of the players from Unionville are still celebrating their championship. Looking around the Horseshoe, I can't help but feel like I have let the opportunity of a lifetime slip away. But then I stop to think about my best friend who has lost his father, and I know that some things mean a lot more than a state championship football game.

CHAPTER 34

December—August

Jack is serious about the possibility of coming to Bertram. He tells me that although winning a state championship is amazing, he wants a fresh start. When I tell the admissions director at Bertram, he is more than excited to find out that Jack wants to transfer in the middle of the year. And after looking into Jack's situation, the school offers him enough financial aid to cover his full tuition. Jack sees it as a great opportunity to get away from so many bad memories in Unionville.

My mom and I have reconciled. I have finally realized that she was doing what she truly believed to be in my best interest. Along with some financial aid, she had gone into her savings fund to pay for tuition during my first year at Bertram. My mother talks to the admissions director and is able to get some additional financial aid for me, too, after explaining that she cannot afford two more years at Bertram. My mom does find a new job as a secretary for an accounting firm, which she says is one hundred times better than working in that factory. She is also going back to school to finish her undergraduate degree.

Taylor comes down to Unionville from Columbus for New Year's Eve, and she and my mom hit it off right away. I can't imagine anyone not liking Taylor. Jack, Taylor, and I go to Mills' Diner and to a late movie, hanging out like three best friends.

In the winter, I play on the junior varsity basketball team, where I get some varsity playing time. That senior class is loaded with great athletes. We end up losing in the state quarterfinals.

I run track for Bertram in the spring, and Jack, after transferring during winter break, pitches for the varsity baseball team. Jack is immediately popular at Bertram. Everyone likes him. He has even started to hang out with Amanda, one of Taylor's best friends from the field hockey team.

And before we know it, our sophomore year is over. My athletic experience is amazing, and my report card is much different from the end of my freshman year at Unionville. I have a B average, and I earn a B+ in Mr. Tanner's English class. What a difference a year makes.

That summer, Jack and I run workouts to prepare for our junior year. Bertram has lost one of its best senior classes ever. Terrance is going to play at Ohio State, and four other seniors will play at Division I schools. Jack and I know that we have our work cut out for us, but we also know that two best friends together can do anything.

While sitting on the football field after a workout, Jack gets this distant look. I wonder if he's thinking about his dad and how things could have been different. The situation is just one of those things that you wish with all your heart hadn't happened.

"You know," Jack says, as he stretches his legs, "my dad sent me a letter before he died. When he had to serve that weekend in jail for his first DUI, he had to write a letter home. Well, he wrote to me."

"What did he say?"

Jack pulls his bag toward him. "You want to read it?"

"Sure, if it's okay with you."

Jack reaches into his bag and pulls out the letter. Obviously, the letter is something that he considers important enough to carry with him. He carefully unfolds the letter, looks it over, and reads through it, pausing for a moment, probably considering whether he wants to share something so personal. Then, he hands me the letter and the envelope.

After examining the letter, I look up at Jack. He nods his head, indicating that it's okay for me to read it. The writing is messy, but I do my best to make out what it says. I begin to read.

Jack,

Part of what I gotta do here is that I have to write this letter to someone in my family. So I picked you. I think I've ruined just about every relationship in my life. For some reason, you've stuck by me. I don't know why, but you have. I wanted to tell you a story, something

that I've never told you before. You know your
Grandpa Joe used to drink a lot. He used to beat
me up pretty good when I was a kid. He would
come home drunk from the bar and take off
his leather belt. When I got older and bigger,
and he was drunk, I used to throw him out of
the house. Your grandma didn't know what to
do, so I would just push him out onto the front
yard and lock the door. While I was growing
up, I told myself I didn't want to be like my
dad. Well, fifteen years later, I failed to become
something else and became exactly like him.
I guess what I'm trying to say is that I don't
want you to be like me. You got so much ability.
I see you running that ball. I see you playing
football and baseball, and I see how you carry
yourself. I don't know how you done so good.
It's real hard for me to say things like this, but
I just want you to know that I'm real proud of
you. I know I'm not real good at showing it. I
wish I didn't mess everything up. I been trying
to get my life back in order. Believe me, I been
trying. If there's one thing I would want you to
do, Son, it is to be something better than me.
My life isn't what I thought it would be. But
you have a chance to make your life something
good. That's what I want for you.
Love, Dad

I look over at Jack, who is wiping the tears from his eyes.

"He loved you," I say.

"Why did this happen?" Jack asks.

Right then, I think about what Leigh said so long ago about the whole world being based on timing. I also think about what Taylor said about there being no mistakes. But when I stand up and reach down to give Jack a lift, I say, "It's a chance."

As we start walking off the field, Jack asks, "A chance to do what?"

"To open your eyes, man. It's a chance to wake up, a chance to break the cycle."

"Break the cycle?" Jack asks.

"Yeah, you have a chance to make your life different from your dad's and your grandfather's. You don't have to end up like them. You don't have to make the same mistakes." I hand the letter and the envelope to Jack.

He takes the letter, folds it, and carefully puts it back in the envelope. He puts it back in his bag and looks at me, saying, "How do I do that? My dad is what I know."

"No, man. You're not like him. You're a winner, and a hard worker. Plus, you've had so many good people around you, so many good role models, like Coach Murphy and Coach Miller. And now you have the people at Bertram, Coach Carlson, and Mr. Tanner."

"But why did it have to happen this way?" Jack asks.

I think back to my conversation with Mr. Tanner after I found out about Jack's father. I think about what he said about losing his best friend in Vietnam. Looking at my own best friend, I say, "Sometimes bad things happen, and there isn't anything we can do about it."

"So how do I get through it?" Jack asks.

I breathe deeply and realize that despite all that's happened with my going to Bertram and leaving my best friends, I have gained a new perspective on life. I feel an energy that I have never felt before. In Unionville, I was with my best friends, people that I cared about and people who cared about me. But with Taylor, and now Jack at Bertram, it's different. Because I'm surrounded by good people and good friends, I feel like I can do anything.

"Do you know how to get through it?" I ask.

Jack looks at me, shakes his head, and says, "No, man. I don't."

Looking at my best friend, I say, "You get through it with the help of your friends. Somebody once told me, a best friend could be the most important thing in the world."

Author Biography

Len Spacek has played or coached just about every sport from college football, to varsity basketball, to middle school track. His purpose for writing *The Final Play* is to get his students interested in reading. At the same time, he wants to demonstrate that sports are about much more than competition and having fun. Sports teach us about life in profound ways. He earned his undergraduate degree from the University of Dayton, his Master's Degree in Education from John Carroll University, and his MFA in Creative Writing from Cleveland State University. He is currently a middle school English teacher. His experiences as a teacher, an athlete, and coach come through in his first novel, *The Final Play*.

Visit his website at www.lenspacek.com

42923746R00152